The Book of Regrets

The Book of Regrets

Compiled by Juliet Solomon

JR
BOOKS

All royalties to The National Hospital for Neurology
and Neurosurgery Development Foundation

Registered Charity No 290173

First published in Great Britain in 2007 by JR Books,
10 Greenland Street, London NW1 0ND
www.jrbooks.com

ISBN 978-1-906217-10-5

1 3 5 7 9 10 8 6 4 2

Printed by MPG Books, Bodmin, Cornwall

Contents

Acknowledgements

This book is dedicated to all the patients who have been treated at the National Hospital for Neurology and Neurosurgery, and their families.

I would like to thank everyone who has helped at various stages of the book; in particular, Cathy Courtney, Jonathan Feldman, Clare Finburgh, Camilla Harney, Andrew Harris, Natasha Harvey, Eileen Hogan, Simon Glazer, Dylan Hearn, Sam, James and Kate Jacobs, Claire Middleditch, Elizabeth Mobayed, Jonathan Moser, Rani and Gary Price, Lisa Silverman, Tania Slowe, Henry Smithson, Minkie Spiro, Lee Stanyer, Brenda Stones, Clare Tunstall, Paddy Walker, Lawrence Webb, and of course my family. Special thanks also to Jeremy Robson, Lesley Wilson and all the team at JR Books.

And finally, my one regret while compiling this book was that on occasion I had to cut short Barney's cherished walks on Hampstead Heath – this will be rectified!

Foreword

Thank you for purchasing *The Book of Regrets*. This book would not have been possible without the tireless work of Juliet Solomon. Juliet's inspiration was simple: what do people regret? Do we more often regret things we have done or things that we haven't done? And do we still regret the things we could go out and rectify? Juliet has compiled a collection of regrets – and lack of regrets – from a fascinating cross-section of people, whose stories she hopes will inspire, and maybe help us all to understand the impact of our choices on ourselves and others.

For many patients and their families the National Hospital for Neurology and Neurosurgery at Queen Square, London, is their last chance: their future depends on the skill of the staff who work to heal the human brain. For many, The National changes lives. With these changes come inevitable shifts in how life is perceived. Regrets lose their aura of disappointment and become inspirational, motivating people to go on to make changes and seek experiences they might otherwise have missed.

Funds raised from *The Book of Regrets* will help the National maintain its position as the leading centre for the diagnosis, treatment and care of patients with a wide range of neurological conditions, including epilepsy, multiple sclerosis, Alzheimer's, stroke and head injuries. Ten million people in the United Kingdom are affected by some kind of neurological condition and the impact is life-changing. The National Hospital Development Foundation (NHDF) is the charity dedicated to supporting the Hospital. The NHDF has raised more than £15 million over the last ten years for cutting-edge equipment, buildings and research.

Our thanks go out to everyone who has taken the time to contribute with such generosity to this book. We have been overwhelmed by the response and the impressive list of contributors is testament to Juliet's hard work and persistence. The stories within are no less remarkable. We hope that you find the book just as entertaining, moving and inspirational as we did.

Christopher Sporborg
Chairman
National Hospital Development Foundation

To find out more about the National Hospital Development Foundation contact:.

National Hospital Development Foundation
Box 123, Queen Square, London WC1N 3BG

Tel: 020 7829 8724
nhdffundraising@uclh.nhs.uk

Visit www.uclh.nhs.uk and click on 'Charities at ULCH'

The NHDF is a Registered Charity No 290173

Introduction

'FOR ALL SAD WORDS OF TONGUE OR PEN, THE SADDEST ARE THESE:
"IT MIGHT HAVE BEEN!"'

JOHN GREENLEAF WHITTIER – AMERICAN QUAKER POET, 1807–1892

'If only....' These must be the two saddest words in the English language, and I have often wondered what regrets people carry around with them through their lives. Does everyone have regrets, or do some people journey through life regretting nothing?

To satisfy this curiosity, I wrote to a number of well-known and successful people in many different walks of life. Embarking on the project, I really wasn't sure what response would follow – would people really want to reflect on their regrets, and would they be prepared to share them publicly in a book, even one for such a great cause? The list of contributors says it all, and the generosity of this many people in taking the time to reply has been overwhelming. The book contains contributions from a wonderfully diverse mix of people. It makes for a truly rich and varied collection – a real treasure trove. Some of the entries are funny, some wistful and some unexpected. A few are extremely moving and personal.

My heartfelt thanks go out to all the contributors who have so kindly supported the National Hospital for Neurology and Neurosurgery.

Juliet Solomon

The Book of Regrets

Michael Parkinson

JOURNALIST AND TV AND RADIO PRESENTER

A couple of years ago I interviewed Clint Eastwood. Twice in a week. The first time was at the National Film Theatre and then on BBC television. I got to know him quite well and apart from admiring him as a great star and director, I came to like him very much indeed. My wife was even more smitten than me. She was totally bowled over by the actor's modesty and easy charm. At the end of the interview I took Mary to Mr Eastwood's dressing room to thank him for doing the show. He said to me: 'I know you love jazz like I do. I have booked a table at Ronnie Scott's; would you and Mary like to join me for some food and good music?' To which I replied, 'I would love to accept but I am very tired and think I will have an early night.' At which point Mary kicked me very hard. Mr Eastwood gave me a quizzical look and said, 'I quite understand.'

It was a month or more before my wife spoke to me again and when she did she wanted to know why anyone who was not completely boring could turn down the chance of dining with Eastwood. Moreover, who in the world would give such a feeble excuse? It might not have been quite my most embarrassing moment, but my wife will take some convincing.

Anne Fine

AUTHOR AND FORMER CHILDREN'S LAUREATE

It seems to me, looking back, that I've spent almost all the waking hours of my life with my nose in a book – either one I'm reading or one I'm writing. I can't honestly say I regret that. (I mean, there's still time to change and I know I won't – ever.)

But I can sincerely regret there weren't more than 24 hours in each day. Because I'd have spent the extra ones on things I know I'd have loved: ice-skating, trampolining, and mucking around in pounding surf on warm sandy beaches.

Oh, yes. And listening to far more music.

Sir Jimmy Savile

FORMER DJ AND TV PRESENTER

My only regret is that I never made a 100 per cent sex symbol!

(I only made 99.9 per cent.)

Ah well.

Prunella Scales

ACTRESS

I regret I never learnt to play the trumpet.

Rowan Williams

ARCHBISHOP OF CANTERBURY

When I was a graduate student in Oxford in the early 1970s, the poet W.H. Auden was in our residence for some of the year, and used to sit every afternoon in a teashop for an hour or so in case students wanted to come to talk to him. I quite often found myself in the same teashop with friends – but never had the nerve to say a word to him. He was by then more than a bit eccentric, and people never quite knew what to expect if they approached him. But most of those who did find the courage were glad they did. When he died unexpectedly, I felt sorry I'd never taken my chance. And over the years, as I came to admire his work more and more, I increasingly cursed my shyness. And I realise that even the most famous of writers will still probably be glad to know that he or she has impressed you.

Tom Conti

ACTOR & AUTHOR

The regrets begin on waking. I regret that I didn't buy batteries for the radio so that I could hear John Humphrys grilling someone that I regret became a politician. Had I bought batteries I would of course regret having listened to John Humphrys and the news because the experience would have filled me with gloom at the state of the State.

In the shower I regret the decision to bury the fittings in the wall because when something goes wrong the whole place has to be torn apart. As I dress I regret that I'm not Cary Grant but console myself that I'm not Ena Sharples. At breakfast I regret not having run five miles because I could now be sitting down to bacon, sausage and eggs instead of the last Ryvita with a bit missing.

In the office I regret that I haven't made more of an effort to replace the wondrous PA who left me, thus proving organised chaos theory. At about four in the afternoon I regret that I've had no lunch. At six, if I'm working in the theatre, I now regret that I'm not filming because I would be two hours away from the end of the working day instead of having to summon the energy, on one cracked Ryvita, to have a snack, shower again, with the same planning regrets I had in the morning, and drive to the theatre, regretting the fact that I'm not in the US where I can fill my petrol tank for £20.

As I slap on the make-up I again regret that I'm not Cary Grant and realise that I am, in fact, metamorphosing into Ena Sharples. As the interval approaches I regret not having insisted on 15 minutes being cut from the first act. In fact, I regret that 15 minutes haven't been cut from every first act ever written.

As I get into bed I regret that it hasn't been arranged, as a special surprise, that Kristin Scott Thomas is in it waiting for me. My two final regrets are that I haven't charged my iPod so that I could listen to Brahms as I fall asleep – and that I didn't buy batteries for my radio so that in the morning I could hear John Humphrys...

All in all, it's been a pretty good day, really.

Katherine Mansfield

AUTHOR 1888–1923

Make it a rule of life never to regret and never

to look back. Regret is an appalling waste

of energy; you can't build on it; it's only good for

wallowing in.

Sir John Major

**PRIME MINISTER AND LEADER
OF THE CONSERVATIVE PARTY, 1990–97**

*I*t is very easy to look back and wish life had been different. I left
school before my 16th birthday – with absolutely no regrets at the
time. But later, I often wondered how differently my life would have
been had I continued my education and gone to university.

And yet, on balance, I learnt a great deal by not doing so. I
learnt what life was like as a manual labourer, as someone who was
unemployed, and as a young banker in Nigeria during the Biafran
War. I saw poverty and hardship on a massive scale and learnt how
lucky I was.

Such experiences left me with no regrets.

Angela Rippon

TV JOURNALIST AND PRESENTER

I regret being too naïve for too long about too many things.

COMEDIAN

Some years ago, about 20 actually, when I was a Charge Nurse at the Maudsley, I had the opportunity to 'rent' an allotment – for £60 a year as I recall – on an exposed hillside overlooking Sydenham Hill golf course (still there). Exposed is not an exaggeration: not only was this an unworked plot for the best part of a century (I do exaggerate), almost impenetrable were the three-foot-high weeds, thistles and nettles, and the 'soil' lay entwined with roots, stones, old boots and assorted debris. The plot benefited from not a bit of shelter, and was open to the elements and at an incline of at least 40 degrees. Just getting up there was a struggle.

However , not to be defeated, I had a great time at Homebase purchasing my spade, fork, rake and dibber, plus a fine assortment of seed crops. I spent a fortune.

And that was about as far as it got. I managed to transfer the gardening accoutrement to my allotted space, much to the amusement of the many elderly gentlemen with horizontal plots, beautifully manicured with a profusion of sprouting seedlings and trellises laden with runner beans and soft fruits. I got there and well, rather gave up.

I regret that a whole range of Wilkinson Sword tools has lain rotting on my patch for the past 20 years, and I deeply regret that I failed to cultivate, to a high horticultural standard, my lovely little space up there on the hillside. Romantic notions that came to nought.

(Fearful that Bob Flowerdew, who torments me every Sunday

afternoon, should ever read this, please insert my contribution under a pseudonym.)

And I'm sure my mother regrets dropping me on my head as a baby; things might have turned out very differently...

≈

ACTOR

———————— ≈ ————————

*P*ersonally, I have more regrets than you have room for in this book, but they are for me to know and for you to leave well alone. Professionally, I have very few, and here is one of them. I have always wanted to do a Western.

When I was a kid, I thought that Cowboys and Indians – as we used to call them in all innocence – had been invented specifically for the silver screen. Their lives seemed so far away from 1950s England, I was really stunned to discover one day that I was seeing a Hollywood version of history! However, this discovery did nothing to dent my romanticised view of the genre, and I still love it. The Western seems to me to offer the perfect formula for a movie – it has everything: natural action, scenery, goodies and baddies. The extremes are built in – it can be hot and dry, snowy or flooded; the stakes are naturally high – territory, property, life itself; and the characters are as big as the country – colourful, eccentric, noble, evil, idealistic and cynical.

My absolute favourite Western is *Once Upon a Time in the West.*

The characters are outrageous, and the story, as well as being rich and complex, touches on something profound in American history. It is fabulously acted, and brilliantly written. And the more I think about it, the more I wish I had had the chance to ride the High Chaparral, round up the herd, light the fire, warm up some coffee and grits, and watch the stars come out. Heigh-ho! Dream on.

Nicholas Hytner

DIRECTOR, NATIONAL THEATRE

Virtually all my regrets concern eyes caught across crowded rooms whose owners I have failed to make any further contact with. I can't believe I'm alone in this.

Matthew Parris

CONSERVATIVE MP '79–86, JOURNALIST & WRITER

It is always things one did not do, opportunities one did not seize, that one regrets. I should have been the first Conservative Member of Parliament, and the first Member of Parliament, to state quite clearly that he was gay. Most people knew anyway, and I had half said it in a speech in the Commons.

I could probably have survived, but out of some misplaced sense of duty not to upset or embarrass my loyal Constituency Association, I stepped back from the challenge. I shall always regret it.

Jeni Barnett

ACTRESS AND TV PRESENTER

At the age of 18 I was encouraged to audition for all the London drama schools. My teacher, Mr Rangeley, believed that I was the new Flora Robson, Peggy Mount and Katherine Ferrier in one small, neurotic body.

I tried RADA, I dried; I tried LAMDA, I faltered; I tried Guildhall and went the way of most starlets; but then I tried the Central School of Speech and Drama. I longed to be in the middle of Swiss Cottage learning how to be Julie Christie or Vanessa Redgrave. I yearned for Louis's patisseries and the haberdashery department in the newly built John Lewis, but the added bonus was that the number 113 bus could get me back to my mother's knishes by sundown.

I arrived at the audition fully prepared. I was shortlisted. I arrived at the second audition fully prepared. But then we had to do movement and my mother's knishes had done their worst.

When a delightful blonde sylph opined that she had left her leotard back in Kingston (that's the one on the A3, not Jamaica), I was happy to offer her mine – newly purchased from the dance shop on the corner of Borehamwood High Street. We came, we danced, she conquered. I was, however, sent to the principal's office.

'We asked you to come fully prepared,' enunciated the high priestess in fully rounded Received Pronunciation.

'We asked you to come fully equipped and you did not. When you are asked to bring a leotard we expect you to bring a leotard. If you wish to succeed in this profession, that is exactly what is needed – professionalism. I am afraid you have not been accepted this time.'

I left crestfallen. The bus ride home was interminable.

Had I kept my leggings to myself, ignored the blonde bird from Kingston and refused my mother's knishes, I would now be on Broadway starring in David Hare's latest play, with a string of Oscars, Baftas and Emmys behind me, not to mention a brother and sister who are icons and a father who was a theatrical luminary.

You see what one black leotard can do.

Chinese proverb

TO REGRET THE PAST
IS TO FORFEIT THE FUTURE.

Major-General Patrick Cordingley

**COMMANDER OF THE DESERT RATS (7TH ARMOURED BRIGADE)
DURING THE FIRST GULF WAR**

---

*T*he place was the Saudi Arabian desert, the date, 27th November 1990. I and my brigade, the Desert Rats, were preparing to attack into Iraq. But on this day we were hosting the British media.

My brief was the first part of their two-day visit and lasted 30 minutes. 'Right,' I said at the end to the two dozen or so journalists in front of me, 'before I hand you over to my chief of staff, Major Euan Loudon, to tell you about the rest of the visit, are there any questions?'

A number came at once, so Chris Sexton stepped in. 'One at a time, please. I'll point to you. Please give your name and the organisation you represent.' All started well with a few innocuous comments. Then trouble began. 'Peter Almond, the *Daily Telegraph*. I wonder if you could tell us your future intentions?'

The one thing that they had all been briefed on was that we were not, under any circumstances, going to discuss future intentions. 'Clearly I can't tell you what the plans are, but I will gladly go over again our training programme and –'

'I don't think we need that again,' another interrupted. 'You must be able to give us some kind of idea as to what is going to happen. We have been told that you could attack into Kuwait soon?'

That line of questioning went on a little longer but got nowhere so eventually I turned the talk round to my concern over trivia. 'I would like to mention, if I may, the role of newspapers in this conflict. The TV reporting, it seems to us, has by and large been very helpful in preparing the nation for a war. It shows us training in a professional fashion and generally concentrates on making serious comments. I don't believe the same is true of the newspapers.'

'David Fairhall, the *Guardian*,' said a grey-haired man. 'On that theme, then, what sort of casualties do you expect that the British public should be prepared for? We have been told in the Ministry of Defence that casualties would be light.' A huge alarm bell should have gone off in my head. It didn't.

'I am quite happy to deal with this because I think it right that the British public should be made aware that a war such as we could fight in the Gulf will result in large numbers of casualties. It is inconceivable that if two armies of the size that are facing each other here went to war, there would not be considerable casualties.' Suddenly all the journalists were scribbling furiously in their notebooks.

I went on: 'Now clearly the majority of casualties will be taken by the loser, and that will be Iraq. Our casualties will be light because we are better trained and better equipped. But whatever, with the power of modern weapon systems there will be casualties to the forward troops and that cannot be avoided.'

Unwittingly I was now right in the middle of a political minefield. They had picked up the trail and were after me. 'What sort of figures are we talking about?' I was pressed. 'What percentage? Two? Ten? Twenty?'

'It's not really possible to put a figure to it,' I said uneasily, sensing where this line of questioning was going.

'We are planning on about fifteen per cent,' interjected Euan. The minefield had just exploded in my face.

'Fifteen per cent!' exclaimed someone from the back. 'That's over one thousand five hundred men from your brigade alone.'

I shot Euan a look that said 'thank you for giving me time but say no more'. I had to set this straight.

'What you must understand is that that is a total figure and most of the casualties will be taken by the Iraqis because of our overwhelming firepower. Don't forget as well that we will win quickly and that means fewer casualties for us. So do keep it in perspective.'

It felt to me that I had extricated myself from the minefield. The scribbling continued, but my points appeared to have been lodged. We had seized back the initiative. And it was time to stop and press on with the visit. I stood up to hand over to Euan.

'Before I go, I hope none of you is going to go away saying that Brigadier Cordingley says there are going to be lots of casualties in the Gulf. That will not help anyone. What we need to do is work out a way of alerting people to the fact that there will be unpleasant things happening if there should be a war and people at home must be prepared for it.'

I walked out of the tent. Chris Sexton followed.

'Blast, that was grim,' I said to Chris. 'What do you think? Are we in trouble?'

'I don't think so, Brigadier,' he said in a way that clearly meant the opposite.

The first hint that something was amiss came with pudding on Thursday 29th. I was eating with the journalists before wishing them goodbye. One lent across the table: 'I'm rather afraid we may not have done you any favours, Brigadier, but I am sure it will be all right.'

What an odd comment to make, I thought. So when Chris took me aside I was already apprehensive.

'We may have a bit of a problem, Brigadier,' he said.

'Oh?' I answered, not wishing to give anything away.

'Yes,' he said and sucked his teeth. 'The headline in tonight's *Evening Standard* reads, "British Commander's warning as Gulf Forces go on Alert: PREPARE FOR A BLOODBATH."'

Oh, how I wish I had kept my mouth shut!

Richard Briers

ACTOR

*H*ow could I have any real regrets – to have survived for 50 years as an actor doing what I always dreamt of doing? Sometimes I regret not having a career as a gardener and living a more quiet and natural life, but I know I would miss the sound of laughter and applause and my ego would start complaining.

Dame Mary Peters

FORMER PENTATHLETE AND OLYMPIC MEDAL WINNER

My mother died when I was 16; I regret her not being alive to be able to share in my sporting success. She was a loving and caring mum, and it would have been nice to have spoilt her.

Alan Sillitoe

AUTHOR

Do I have any regrets? Yes, of course, but nothing too serious. I regret that I didn't become a radio officer in the Merchant Marine when I left the RAF at 21. I regret that I don't have more than one life, or that I can't live forever and go on writing novels. Yet I have had two lives: one before becoming a writer, and one afterwards, which I more or less got sidetracked into through having picked up tuberculosis in Malaya. I also could say I regret not becoming a land surveyor. And yet I look upon regrets as vain because Fate makes us all, and we have to take what it dishes out.

Kahlil Gibran

ARTIST, POET AND WRITER 1883–1931

The chemist who can extract from his heart's elements compassion, respect, longing, patience, regret, surprise, and forgiveness and compound them into one can create that atom which is called love.

Oliver Sacks

NEUROLOGIST AND AUTHOR

I have innumerable regrets – many inadmissible and unpublishable! Although, mercifully, they are counterbalanced by the things for which I am grateful.

Dannie Abse

POET AND AUTHOR

*B*ecause of the car accident during the night of 13 June 2005 when my wife was killed, I regret many things. Not least that I didn't arrive on the M4 one minute earlier or later. In rare moments when I forget to be grateful that, physically, I suffered only minor injuries, I regret that I managed to crawl out of the capsized car alive. But mostly I regret commonplace things: that I didn't help my wife enough with household tasks and with shopping, etc. And perhaps, during our many decades of a happy marriage, I should have told her that I loved her even more often than I did!

I intended to write a poem for this book. I tried, but the words wouldn't arrive in the right order. I regret that this is so.

Michael Morpurgo

AUTHOR AND CHILDREN'S LAUREATE, 2003–5

I haven't: played rugby for England.
Lived by the sea.
Seen a giraffe in the wild.
Met Mozart or Mandela.
Stood on top of the world.
Soared like an eagle.
Written as wonderfully as Robert Louis Stevenson or
Ted Hughes (but I'm working on it).

Nicholas Parsons

ACTOR AND RADIO AND TV PRESENTER

I have always regretted those occasions when, while playing in an important cricket match, I decided to try and strike the ball to the boundary, when it would have been wiser to have left it or played defensively – as a result I am out before making a reasonable score.

Terry Waite

FORMER CHURCH OF ENGLAND ENVOY & HUMANITARIAN

I was very fond of my grandmother although I saw her only infrequently. She lived over 30 miles from our home and the only possible way I could get to see her was by bicycle. Public transport was then as it is today – virtually non-existent.

I would leave home early in the morning on a bicycle that my father had assembled for me. He had a second-hand frame sprayed blue at the local garage and collected the other parts where and when he could. I would arrive at my grandmother's house mid-morning. In winter there was always a cheerful coal fire blazing in the hearth and I would settle myself by it as she told me stories of times past.

Life had not been easy for her. During the years following the First World War my grandfather's business had failed and she was faced with the daunting task of feeding and clothing six children. Fortunately she had received a good musical education and could take in students who were anxious to learn to play the piano. Alas, this activity did not provide enough to balance the books and so she applied to the local cinema for work as a pianist. Those were the days of the silent films and her job was to keep one eye on the screen and the other on the keyboard and improvise for all she was worth.

In the corner of her living room sat an upright piano. After lunch with my grandfather, a giant of a man with a fine white beard, we would return to the parlour and I would ask her to play for me. She began with Chopin and Beethoven and as a grand finale I would always request that she played the music of the silent films. I can see her now as her eyes sparkled and her hands flew across the keys. She was a natural musician.

'You must learn to play, Terry,' she would say as she attempted to explain to me the mysteries of a musical score. 'You have a natural touch and would make a good pianist.'

Alas, it was not to be. The distance between our two houses was too great to allow for regular lessons and a piano was way beyond the pocket of my father, a village policeman.

As I recollect days long past, I am probably older than my grandmother was when she played for me during a winter afternoon. I have loved music all my life and many is the time I have longed to be able to sit down and play as effortlessly as my grandmother did.

It was not to be.

When I was taken into captivity many years ago I said to myself, 'No regrets, no self-pity and no over-sentimentality.' Then, I would not allow myself to regret, but now I can admit to this one. Yes, there are others but they are for another time.

Lord Ashdown

FORMER LEADER OF THE LIBERAL DEMOCRAT PARTY

One of my great regrets is that I gave up the piano despite the admonitions of my mother at the age of 11.

Sir Winston Churchill

FORMER BRITISH PRIME MINISTER 1874–1965

———— ⧈ ————

I must place on record my regret that the human
race ever learned to fly.

⧈

Ian Appleby

**CONSULTANT NEUROANAESTHETIST, NATIONAL HOSPITAL
FOR NEUROLOGY AND NEUROSURGERY**

My two greatest passions have always been sport and music.
My interview for medical school consisted entirely of questions such as 'What position do you play?' and 'Could you play centre/fly-half if needed?' I've made countless friends, experienced the elation and despair that every 'sportsman' knows, and travelled extensively on the back of some moderate ability to play ball sports. Like every sportsman, I've dreamt of scoring the Cup Final winning goal – for Newcastle – at Wembley, kicking the penalty

in the dying seconds at Twickenham, hooking Glenn McGrath for six – and because I'd played sport to a reasonable level, I could see that these dreams would remain just that and get on with enjoying my level of competition.

Music, however, was always different. I had absolutely no talent for any musical instrument but I listened to music every day – and still do. Every journey into the hospital, in my office, in the operating theatre – always music. And the thing that most fascinates me is how there is a particular piece of music for every mood, feeling and emotion I've ever had. Of all the music that I listen to, there is one piece that I come back to time and time again. In the space of 42 minutes it encapsulates all life, simple as that. It is 'Dark Side of the Moon' by Pink Floyd. Every time I listen to it I wish I'd been able to play an instrument, sing, do anything to have been able to create something so special. So, my only regrets are that I wasn't born about 10 years earlier, that I didn't play the drums, that I went to St Barts Medical School and not Central Saint Martins, and that somewhere along the line I wasn't asked to take Nick Mason's place in Pink Floyd!

Yvonne Brewster

THEATRE DIRECTOR & WRITER

'Latin is a dead language,

As dead as dead can be.

It killed the ancient Romans,

And now it's killing me.'

This was the fourth-form chant we used to taunt Miss Nation, teacher of Latin. It rang out loudly at her receding back, which was too new and too timid to turn around and give the order mark this behaviour merited.

Problem was, I took this pathetic rite of passage a step too far and walked away from Miss Nation's Latin class the moment it was possible. Regrets, I have a few – but my lack of Latin is one of the most enduring… The real joy of appreciating Romance languages in depth lost, because of such silly schoolgirl bravado.

Sir Terence Conran

DESIGNER AND RESTAURATEUR

When I review my regrets, they are so egotistical that I would hate to see them consigned to print. On the whole I have had a fantastic life with many opportunities, most of which have materialised.

My only real regrets are friends who have died – although I do wish I had taken more exercise when I was younger as I have a very bad back, which is exhausting.

Sir Victor Blank

CHAIRMAN, LLOYD'S TSB

In a working life spanning nearly half a century, I have been a shop assistant, a solicitor, a merchant banker, a newspaper man, a retailer and now the chairman of a major bank. As a career, I would not change any of it and still count my blessings and good fortune daily. But, of course, there are some regrets. One, that must be shared by almost everybody who has worked or today works in the City, is that the work–life balance is difficult to maintain in good order. I would love to have had more time at home with children who have become adults all too quickly. And secondly, I have never understood why the England cricket selectors overlooked my talents. Having clean bowled Clive Lloyd and hit Shane Warne to the boundary fence in my fifties, how could such talent have been missed? But I can still dream on!

Lord Hattersley

FORMER DEPUTY LEADER OF THE LABOUR PARTY 1983–92

I have only two regrets. The first is that I did not own a dog for 20 years of my life. The second is that I do not enjoy an inferior television programme called *Murder, She Wrote*. Were that to give me pleasure I could be happy for the rest of my life, as repeats appear on television for 25 hours a day.

Patricia Greene

PLAYS JILL ARCHER IN *THE ARCHERS*

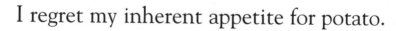

I regret my inherent appetite for potato.

Benjamin Zephaniah

POET

A long time go when I was very, very young, I wrote a letter to Bob Marley. I told him I was a poet and wanted to know what he thought of the six poems that I had enclosed. I was so happy when he wrote back and told me that Britain needs me and that I should keep writing. I met him a few years later and I was amazed when he remembered me; I was even more amazed when he was able to quote some of my poetry back to me. Since then I try to answer all letters that are sent to me because I know how much this can mean to the writers of these letters.

My biggest regret is that I didn't keep his handwritten reply to me. I just didn't think. I read it, showed it to a few friends, and put it in the bin. People keep telling me that it would be so valuable now, but I don't care about the money – for me it would have been of great personal value.

Later on in life, after the death of Bob Marley, I was lucky enough to go to Jamaica and work with his band, The Wailers. That was also a great moment.

Bob Marley actually sat down and took the time to write a letter to me. I really regret throwing that letter away, but at least I now have a record credited to Benjamin Zephaniah and the Wailers. Sometimes I listen to that recording and I'm sure I can hear brother Bob singing in the background.

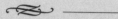

François de la Rochefoucauld

AUTHOR 1613–1680

Sometimes we lose friends for whose loss our regret is greater than our grief, and others for whom our grief is greater than our regret.

Dame Beryl Bainbridge

AUTHOR

The thing I regret most is my attitude to my mother, Winnie, once she grew old. It was alright to be rebellious and scornful of her views when I was growing up; that's the only way the young can break free. But I didn't understand about old age. She lived in Liverpool and I lived in London, and though she came to stay with me regularly and I telephoned her twice a week, I had no idea of what she was going through. When we did meet it was only a matter of hours before I became exasperated by her apparent deafness, her nodding off in the afternoon, her constant remembrances of times past, and her forgetfulness as to where she'd left her spectacles, her keys, her library book.

Now that I too am growing old, and subjecting my own children to such irritations, I am aware of how selflessly they treat me; they look for the keys, shout a bit louder, appear interested when I spout on about the War and how I was put to bed under the dining room table when the May Blitz began. My mum died in bed, alone, 33 years ago.

My other regret is the treatment I gave my two cats, Pudding and her son Gerald. I say they were mine, though in theory they were bought at the insistence of my children who, once they'd left home, had nothing to do with them. Pudding was a rotten mother and hated Gerald. When he sat on the ground-floor windowsill she would leap across from the steps and knock him into the basement area below; consequently, he was a little stupid.

Pudding had given birth, secretly, to a previous litter. When I was cleaning out the wardrobe 10 years later I came across the mummified remains of five kittens. That says something about Pudding and even more about me. She and Gerald lived for almost 20 years, and during the last five I rarely allowed them into the house. It was all a long time ago, but sometimes, in daydreams, I hear them mewing.

Brendan Foster

FORMER DISTANCE RUNNER AND OLYMPIC MEDAL WINNER

My biggest regret is that I was not a better footballer. My biggest dream would have been to play the centre forward position for Newcastle United Football Club and play in the same team as Jackie Milburn and Alan Shearer.

Una Stubbs

ACTRESS

I regret very much not having been more confrontational during my life. This is such a main regret that all others pale into insignificance.

Mark Twain

AUTHOR 1835–1910

Why was the human race created? Or at least why wasn't something creditable created in place of it? God had His opportunity. He could have made a reputation. But no, He must commit this grotesque folly – a lark which must have cost Him a regret or two when He came to think it over and observe effects.

Ann Daniels

POLAR EXPLORER

here are over 500 miles of moving snow and ice between Canada and the Geographic North Pole. Temperatures can be as low as -48° and there is only a small chance of success; many expeditions have tried and failed to reach the Pole. In 2002, when I put together what was to become the first all-women's team to walk to the South and North Pole, the decision was made not to take toilet paper on the expedition to the North Pole. Every piece of equipment, together with food and fuel, has to be hauled to the Pole in huge sledges and weight is a crucial factor in success or failure. Anything that was not needed for survival or did not contribute directly to the success of the journey was ejected. All wrappers were removed, there was no soap, deodorant, books or music, and no toilet paper.

Unfortunately, for the first 27 days, we were subject to the most appalling temperatures and conditions. The terrain was monstrous and we were hit by three storms, one so severe that we couldn't erect the tent and had to huddle under the material for three days with little food and water. Every member of the team suffered frostbite to some degree. Pom's toes were particularly bad and Caroline had frostbitten fingers. This meant that for a few days Caroline could not use her hands very well, couldn't expose them to the elements outside and most certainly couldn't handle snow wedges to clean her bottom. As the one person on the expedition who has children, I was used to taking care of people who had difficulty dressing themselves. I was happy to tie boot laces, overjoyed to fasten harnesses and ski bindings and zip up jackets, but my one regret during the whole expedition was the decision *not to take toilet paper.*

Antony Worrall Thompson

CHEF AND RESTAURATEUR

I regret having been so impulsive in the choice of my early wives. It's only when you meet the 'real' person that you know what real love is. It's a lesson I've taken into my more mature life: 'Think before you act, pace yourself, take your time, don't always strike while the iron is hot'.

Nobby Stiles

FORMER MANCHESTER UNITED & ENGLAND FOOTBALL PLAYER

My first memory of football was listening to the 1948 FA Cup when Manchester United beat Blackpool.

My ambition was to become a United player and play at Wembley in a Cup final. Unfortunately, I played in several semi-finals in the 1960s but never reached the final. I received a winner's medal in 1963, but I didn't play when United beat Leicester City 3–1 in that year's FA Cup final. Other than that, no regrets.

Gervase Phinn

AUTHOR

If I had another chance at being a father

I would listen more readily to my children,

Take more risks, visit more places,

Sing more songs, play more games,

Watch more sunsets and read more stories with them,

And I would never miss an opportunity to say a kind word.

If I had another chance at being a father

I would take myself less seriously,

Laugh with my children more and moan at them less,

Answer their questions with greater honesty,

And I should tell them each day of their young lives

Just how much I love them.

Jon Ronson

AUTHOR AND DOCUMENTARY FILM-MAKER

*n*ot so long ago I received a telephone call out of the blue from Robbie Williams. He had read one of my books – *Them: Adventures with Extremists* – and had quoted parts of it on stage to 60,000 fans in Antwerp. I found this incredibly exciting. For two years we spoke about the idea of doing a book and documentary together in which we would travel the world solving mysteries, like Mulder and Scully, or Dangermouse and Penfold. I set up a fantastic trip for us. Then, at the last minute, Robbie decided he didn't want to do it. He was just out of rehab and was, he said, 'happily agoraphobic' at his house in Los Angeles.

My regret is that my epic, funny, strange, moving, surreal, unexpected, frightening, exciting journey with Robbie Williams is an adventure that won't be had and a book that won't be written.

Patrick Cox
SHOE DESIGNER

My biggest regret is not registering the name 'Wannabe'. I am a shoe designer and way back in 1993 I drew a cute loafer which was an instant success and very rapidly started to sell in big numbers, and so, working with an Italian manufacturer, I spun it off into its own 'Wannabe' collection and let them register the name. Doh! The rest is history…

Virginia Ironside
AGONY AUNT, BROADCASTER AND AUTHOR

On the outside, I've had a very fortunate and successful life. I've written several books and have the most wonderful family whom I love dearly. My greatest regret, however, is that I ever allowed myself to be born. I think I am speaking for a large minority of people, who dare not admit this truth in public, when I say that for us no amount of love or success can make up for the wretched business of living, the huge and daily effort, the presence of a fundamental hopelessness, loss and grief that lies permanently at our core.

Karim Brohi

**CONSULTANT TRAUMA SURGEON,
BARTS AND THE LONDON NHS TRUST**

T hey always attack in the morning, when I'm half-awake and at my most vulnerable. Not every morning by any means, and it doesn't seem to make a difference whether it's a work day and I'm late, or I slept in on a lazy weekend. But they always, always get me when I'm brushing my teeth. I look up from the sink, catch sight of myself in the mirror and get smacked straight in the face.

It doesn't matter whether it's something inappropriate I said in a meeting the day before or diving into the swimming pool without putting my swimming trunks on when I was eight years old (my earliest I think), not kissing the girl who played clarinet in second orchestra or choosing the wrong path on one of those big, life-changing, one-way decisions. During a toothbrush moment the effect is the same – the brush pauses somewhere over my second molar, eyes lock with my reflection's and I wince as the shame, pain and regret hit and everything comes flooding back, relived in the moment. Time passes and eventually my right arm aches; I shake my head in regret, and carry on brushing.

I have no idea why regrets always pick this time to surface, but if you have enough toothbrush moments it makes you think twice about brushing in the morning.

BROADCASTER

---- ~ ----

I very much regret that I have never learnt to speak another language. I feel so 'out of it' when I'm abroad, particularly in France, as it should have been possible for me to learn French.

~

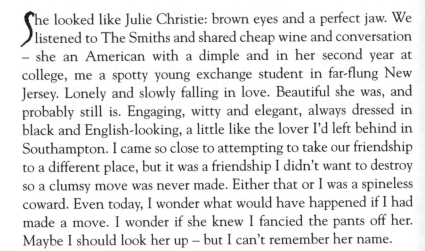

ASSOCIATE EDITOR, *THE SUN*

---- ~ ----

*S*he looked like Julie Christie: brown eyes and a perfect jaw. We listened to The Smiths and shared cheap wine and conversation – she an American with a dimple and in her second year at college, me a spotty young exchange student in far-flung New Jersey. Lonely and slowly falling in love. Beautiful she was, and probably still is. Engaging, witty and elegant, always dressed in black and English-looking, a little like the lover I'd left behind in Southampton. I came so close to attempting to take our friendship to a different place, but it was a friendship I didn't want to destroy so a clumsy move was never made. Either that or I was a spineless coward. Even today, I wonder what would have happened if I had made a move. I wonder if she knew I fancied the pants off her. Maybe I should look her up – but I can't remember her name.

Katharine Hepburn

ACTRESS 1907–2003

I have many regrets, and I'm sure
everyone does. The stupid things
you do, you regret, if you have
any sense, and if you don't regret
them, maybe you're stupid.

Lord Stevenson

BUSINESSMAN AND CHAIR OF THE HOUSE OF LORDS APPOINTMENTS COMMISSION

I deeply regret not having had more courage and throwing myself into sports when I was younger. I now realise that while never exactly world-champion class at any sport, I was much better than I gave myself credit for but was too shy and frightened. I also regret giving up the piano when I was about 10. Although I kept up the violin – and still play – music would be an infinitely greater source of pleasure had I continued.

It's difficult to think of many other regrets about things I have missed out on – I have led a very lucky life and have been included rather than excluded. By contrast, there are so many things I wish I had done differently or better.

I wish I had understood at an earlier age that business – indeed, everything – is more about people than it is about analysis, money or anything else. It would have saved me a lot of angst and misunderstanding.

And I deeply regret that I admitted to my wife how much colder my native Scotland is than her homeland of Suffolk!

Libby Purves

BROADCASTER AND JOURNALIST

When I was at school in France for three years, my father being a consul posted to Lille, I used to go ice-skating every Sunday with my friend Véronique Thiriez. I was 11, and I went alone on the tram with my skates in a bag – I can still see its shape and feel its weight now.

Véronique was a good skater, and encouraged me to move away from the rail and get into that gliding open-toed rhythm, and to learn (as one does on a bicycle) that stability can only be achieved at a certain speed. So that what feels less safe is, in fact, more safe.

One of the tunes they played incessantly then, back in the 1960s, was Edith Piaf's 'Je Ne Regrette Rien'. Taken all together, the speed of my circuits, the rush of cool ice-air against my face, the exhilaration of the words and the brash sound of Piaf taught me something. They taught me not to regret the falls, the bumps and the awkward clutchings at the rail when I lost the rhythm or my ankles gave way. Better to skate fast and smoothly, to let go of the rail and lose, than to stand wobbling like a coward on the edge of life. It was one of those unspoken life-lessons that you don't realise are lessons at all, until years later.

I probably owe whatever nerve I have ever displayed partly to ice, and to Piaf. It has been a small part of every job I have left for something new and riskier, every plain word I have said despite the risk of mockery, every encouragement I gave my children to sail and ride and dive and be brave, however nervous it made their mother.

So it is ironic that one of my great regrets is that I gave up skating just when I was getting reasonably good at it, and grew into a cautious shuffling tubby adult who hates the idea of falling over!

Geoffrey Raisman

PROFESSOR OF NEUROSCIENCE AND HEAD OF THE SPINAL REPAIR UNIT, INSTITUTE OF NEUROLOGY

*T*here are positive regrets for things done, and negative regrets for things missed. My list would be so long it would reach the heavens in mute reproach...

Being able to sing? That would have been wonderful for giving lectures and calming savage breasts and conquering more hearts, especially when the vast majority of people can sing and don't ever use the faculty.

Chris Parker

PLAYED SPENCER MOON IN *EASTENDERS*

*S*ome people say that it is wrong to have regrets. I disagree. Regrets can prompt you to make amends. My biggest regret is not travelling. Many of my friends have taken sabbaticals and gap years to go travelling and the stories, pictures, friends and experiences that they return with seem to really change their outlook. OK, so it can get annoying when you are stuck at work reading a group email from a friend who is laying on a beach in Thailand while on their 'travels'...but do something about it! It is harder for me to take a break now to travel than it was when I was 16, but I am going to do something about it – I'm saving my air miles and I'm going to go backpacking before it's too late!

Paul Daniels

MAGICIAN

*U*ntil very recently I never felt the emotion of 'regretting'. To be honest I could not see the point of it. I have made mistakes (although I would never confess that to Debbie, my wife, who might gloat over my imperfection) and I have 'lost' moments of opportunity, but at the back of my mind has always been the feeling that regret would not put the mistakes right or bring those moments back again. I just got on with living.

A journalist did ask about regrets recently and with a blinding flash one came. I wish I had not wasted (and I really do mean wasted or given away) my money on flashy and expensive cars. At the end of the day a car is a metal box with a wheel in each corner and gets you from A to B. The price rises enormously if you go for what they call a 'marque', which turns out to be something that Jeremy Clarkson eulogises over but in the reality of our roads doesn't get you there any quicker and only slightly more comfortably. The initial cost and the running expenses of these metal boxes are gross and I have resolved not to fall for the marketing expertise ever again. If I do, I'll regret it.

Corin Redgrave

ACTOR

I regret that I never played Hamlet and I never had a brother.

Ian Rickson

FORMER ARTISTIC DIRECTOR, ROYAL COURT THEATRE

I regret loneliness as a teenager. Not being braver at reaching out to people. Connecting, yielding… But it may have made me appreciate my life more, now.

Jeremy Irons

ACTOR

Eleven years ago I had one dog, an old mutt called Flyer, whom I had collected 11 years earlier from Battersea Dogs Home. Then a stray came into my life, a little black water dog I called Skitter.

She produced three puppies before sadly drowning, leaving me with the two bitches and one dog. I gave the dog away and he is now the scourge of Hampstead Heath, but the two bitches I kept and because of their randy father, felt I should spay them, which I did. Eventually the father died and my two dogs have developed into extraordinary companions. I would love to breed from them to start a line, but since they are spayed, I cannot. This is a big regret.

COMEDIAN

I regret that I didn't:

Kiss enough girls

Become a rock star

Learn to cook rice properly

Listen to my elders

Become the Olympic high-jump champion

See Jacques Brel in concert

Find something to believe in

Tell the people who I love how I feel

Like *The West Wing*

Move to America on the back of *Trigger Happy
TV* and become a multi-millionaire.

I regret that I did:

Make someone cry

Become a Goth

Move to the BBC

Buy the flat below me

Kill a man in Morocco

Take up origami

Visit Finland

Have a phase wearing skirts

Kill a robin with a catapult

More harm than good.

Sir Patrick Moore

ASTRONOMER AND AUTHOR

I have been lucky – I am an astronomer and author, and these are also my interests, so I have never had to 'work' in the accepted meaning of the term. But one thing I regret. Since a small boy I have composed music – marches and waltzes, etc. For example, I wrote the march 'Out of the Sky' for the band of the Royal Parachute Brigade, and it is one of their regular marches (I heard them playing it, on the radio, the other day). I have also written xylophone music (in 1982 I played one of my xylophone solos at the Royal Command Performance). I am conceited enough to think that I could have made a name as a composer, but I simply did not have the time to pay real attention to it, and as I am now 84 it is a little late to try! At least I have left one CD of my compositions…

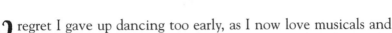

Lesley Joseph

ACTRESS

I regret I gave up dancing too early, as I now love musicals and really would love to kick my leg up high with the best of them.

I regret I didn't learn to sing properly.

I regret my teenage arrogance that I knew best and no one else could tell me what to do. I regret I didn't travel the world when I had the chance.

I regret I didn't realise that everyone feels little inside, and that I am as good as the next person, but that is something you only learn with experience.

But thinking again – my life is pretty goddamned good, so I'm going to enjoy what I have, because what is the point of regretting? It's too late now.

Prue Leith

RESTAURATEUR AND COOKERY WRITER

'Je ne regrette rien'…except perhaps
that I never learnt to sing.

Sir Jonathon Porritt

**ENVIRONMENTALIST AND FORMER CHAIRMAN OF
THE GREEN PARTY**

I really regret having bottled out of taking science seriously when I was at school. For some reason, I just made up mind that I wasn't any good at it, that it was too hard, and it wasn't going to help me in later life – so why bother?

It certainly bothers me now! I've been involved in environmental issues of one kind or another for more than 30 years, and a lot of them depend on controversial and often complex scientific information and elements. As a result I have to work very hard indeed to keep up to speed – and it doesn't come naturally. Hugging trees has always been so much easier than grappling with the process of photosynthesis!

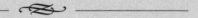

Chuang Tzu

CHINESE PHILOSOPHER 399–286BC

The perfect man uses his mind as a mirror. It grasps nothing. It regrets nothing. It receives but does not keep.

Mark Lawrenson

**FOOTBALL COMMENTATOR AND FORMER
LIVERPOOL & IRELAND FOOTBALLER**

---

ike many people, if I could turn back the clock I arguably would do so. However, I am of the belief that fate plays a major role in our lives and the decisions we take are for a reason. But I do have one major regret – not since the age of 18 have I had my own front teeth!

In 1975 I was a young professional footballer playing for my beloved Preston North End versus Grimsby Town in a Division 2 fixture. As a fledgling centre-back I was always told to impose myself on the opposition centre-forward, which I did on numerous occasions during the game, by virtue of some hefty tackles on someone who had a definite physical advantage over yours truly. On the last of these challenges, I was given by my opponent what can only be described as a 'knowing look'.

Eventually, when Grimsby earned a corner, I got myself in a good position to be able to see the ball. When the kicker delivered it, the realisation that the ball was about to land in my area, and I had to deal with it, meant I kept my eyes firmly focused to head the corner away to safety. I did. But at the crucial moment of contact, I tasted a big fat Grimsby elbow. Bye bye, teeth!

Fergal Keane

BROADCASTER & JOURNALIST

I have a few regrets. They mostly have to do with how I've treated other people, the times I acted out of selfishness or fear, and times when I let people down. One can only try to make amends as best as one can on a daily basis.

Lord Tebbit

CONSERVATIVE PARTY MP AND FORMER CABINET MINISTER

One of the greatest regrets of my life is that on 12 October 1984 my wife decided that rather than heading for home in Devon that night, we would stay on in Brighton to be on the platform the next day for the Prime Minister's speech at the Conservative Party Conference.

Matthew Walker

PROFESSOR OF NEUROLOGY, INSTITUTE OF NEUROLOGY

I regret being old enough to have regrets.

Peter Shilton

FORMER NOTTINGHAM FOREST AND ENGLAND GOALKEEPER

One of the biggest regrets I have in my football career is not to have won an FA Cup winners' medal. It was the only major trophy to elude me.

Being a Leicester-born boy I was brought up on FA Cup defeats with Leicester City having lost three in a row, in 1949, 1961 and 1963. I went to the 1963 final, stood behind the goal and watched in tears as we lost 3–1 to Manchester United. The nearest I came to winning the medal was in 1969 when I played for Leicester and we lost to Manchester City 1–0 in a game we should have won.

I think I was fated not to win the FA Cup.

Martha Kearney

JOURNALIST & BROADCASTER

One of my biggest regrets is that I didn't have a more adventurous gap year. None of my friends had taken the same time off so I didn't have a travelling companion. My parents had just moved to the United States, so I spent nine months at home, watching bad TV, eating ice cream, doing temp jobs, smoking and not doing my preparation reading for university. It was a waste, really. I was very jealous when I got to Oxford and found everyone else had trekked overland to India or lived on a kibbutz. I did finally get my year back-packing, aged 30, and loved travelling through South America and India.

Kenneth Clarke

CONSERVATIVE PARTY MP AND FORMER CABINET MINISTER

I think that politicians should never admit their mistakes or express regrets because, contrary to popular belief, their opponents and the press never cease to deride them when they do!

However, I will admit that I do regret having been responsible, when I was a junior minister for transport, for inflicting road humps on the country's roads. It was a good idea to have the occasional speed hump in a residential back street, to restrain the speed of people taking rat runs. However, I never expected to find myself driving over thousands of them all over the country on main roads and minor ones. There is one every 100 yards on a street near where I live, and every time my bones are shaken, I curse my error!

Jimmy Hill

FORMER FOOTBALLER, MANAGER AND TV PERSONALITY

I was Chairman of the Professional Footballers' Association (PFA) from 1957 to 1961, and when I was playing I never earned more than £20 per week plus £2 for a win and £1 for a draw. I was able in 1961 to get the maximum wage eliminated. Unfortunately, I lost the second cartilage in my right leg and had to give up playing. But, fortunately, I was able to get a job as a manager on the other side of the football fence.

However, having removed the maximum wage as Chairman of the PFA, I then found myself having to negotiate with players and their agents to establish how much to pay them once I had become a manager. I suppose one can't win 'em all! My only regret is that the majority of clubs under pressure from fans pay far more than they can afford.

Hugh Dennis

COMEDIAN

I don't really have that many regrets. Not because I have led a charmed life in which I have always made the right choices, but rather because, as a comedian, I have always known that every disaster is a potential anecdote. It may, of course, be too painful to tell for a while afterwards but eventually at some point, perhaps on stage, perhaps at a dinner party, its time will come, and with the details exaggerated and the names changed, the pain of the remembered episode will be used for the purpose of entertainment.

I should, for example, have regretted my decision at the age of 18 to stand on the ninth green at Stanmore golf course while my friend Bryn sent a somewhat wayward shot skyward with his eight-iron. I should have regretted it because the ball hit me on the head, splitting it open, knocking me down and leaving me bleeding on the green. And yet somehow, even as the ball bounced off my partially exposed skull to within one foot of the flag, I knew that it would be a story; and so did Bryn, a story to which he then gave the requisite twist by refusing to take me to hospital until he had putted for a rather unexpected birdie.

Likewise I should regret getting a Grade E in my Physics A-Level, and it did seem disastrous at the time, making entry to my first-choice university rather less likely. Yet had I not got that grade I would never have uncovered the story of Andy – a boy in the year above – who had taken his A-Levels twice. The first time he got two O grades and an F (Fail). In the re-takes he got two

F grades and an O. Disaster? Oh no, not a bit of it. He was delighted because now he could spell 'Oo, F Off' with his A-Level results.

Nor at Cambridge, where I ended up in spite of my Physics disaster, would I have fully appreciated the attitude of my friend Paul as he stood in front of the board of the Senate House where the finals results were posted. He had got a 2:2 and looked enormously depressed. Those with him tried to comfort him.

'It's OK, Paul. It's not a first, it may not be a 2:1, but it's also not a third.'

'Yes, but that is just it,' said Paul, 'I now realise I could have worked less hard.'

And medically there are things I should also regret, but don't. Last year I had to have a colonoscopy and chose to go locally for what is essentially a humiliating but straightforward procedure. And there was nothing to make me doubt the wisdom of my choice until the doctor, by now poised above me ready to insert the tube into my fully exposed and evacuated posterior, turned to me, smiled, and said, 'I'm a very good friend of your next-door neighbour.'

To paraphrase Sinatra: 'Regrets, I've had a few. But then again, enough to mention.'

M.R.D. Foot

HISTORIAN AND AUTHOR

Between school and Oxford in 1938 I got as far as Istanbul, where I was bowled over by the church of Santa Sophia. All its interior except the pendentives of the great dome had been covered in whitewash. While revelling in the wonders of its architecture, I met an older American who showed me in the narthex what he had been allowed to uncover.

It was a magnificent sixth-century mosaic of Christ and his mother, simply inscribed as 'MP ΘY'. Could I read the inscription? Of course I could. Had I Latin as well as Greek? How else had I got into Oxford? *Would I care to be his secretary?*

I reckoned I would make Professor Whittemore (to whom I turned out to be talking) a better secretary if I had a degree. He agreed; so I missed my chance to help him uncover the rest of those marvellous mosaics. Yet, had I stayed there, I would certainly have joined someone's secret service in the impending war; and I was then so brash that I would surely have ended up, quite promptly, in a sack in the Bosphorus, tied tight at the neck.

FORMER CHAMPION JOCKEY

My main regret is not winning the Champion Chase at Cheltenham; I was upsided at the last fence on seven different occasions.

MOUNTAINEER AND ADVENTURER

I have tried to live my life with no regrets as my philosophy is: one can do nothing about the past; live for the present and don't worry about the future. If I have ever thought about something I have inevitably gone ahead and done it. Some jobs, races and adventures have been more successful than others, but that's life!

However, I do have one regret and that is not spending more time studying languages. Dentistry has been my job for over 20 years, but adventure has been my passion. My adventures have taken me to some of the most amazing places on this beautiful planet we live on. The people I have met have been fantastic and I would have loved to have been able to communicate in their native tongue – even though, as I have frequently found out, language is not always needed to communicate. I have just climbed Mount Everest with 14 Russian climbers – an amazing trip but I did not speak Russian and most of the Russians did not speak English. So I had an interesting time but 10 weeks of very limited talking, and those people who know me will appreciate that that was agony for me as I'm not the most quiet and retiring person around (and I still haven't kissed the Blarney stone)!

However, there is one thing I can ask for in a number of languages and that is my shoe size – information which most ladies know!

Anton Chekhov

AUTHOR AND PLAYWRIGHT 1860–1904

The people I am afraid of are the ones who look for tendentiousness between the lines and are determined to see me as either liberal or conservative. I am neither liberal, nor conservative, nor gradualist, nor monk, nor indifferentist. I would like to be a free artist and nothing else, and I regret God has not given me the strength to be one.

Neil Kitchen

CONSULTANT NEUROSURGEON, NATIONAL HOSPITAL FOR NEUROLOGY AND NEUROSURGERY

I regret a lot:

> not waiting an extra five minutes during that operation last week
>
> not double-checking the brain scans done today
>
> not seeing my patient before going home
>
> not being clear enough in outpatients
>
> not telling bad news kindly
>
> not remembering to talk to relatives as promised
>
> not bothering...

A doctor who doesn't regret doesn't care. We are imperfect and we need to continue to learn to regret, to improve our patient care.

Sir Christopher Frayling

CHAIRMAN OF THE ARTS COUNCIL

Someone once observed that no one ever said as their last words, 'I wish I'd spent more time at the office.' As someone who spends an awful lot of time at meetings, on committees and generally 'at the office', I tend to agree with this. I also instinctively tend to distrust people who join in with Edith Piaf's 'Je Ne Regrette Rien' with a smug look on their face, and ditto Frank Sinatra's 'My Way'. Unless, that is, the song is sung by Sid Vicious, in which case the words completely change their meaning, from smugness to Sid-against-the-world.

Anyway, here goes. When I was at university I spent a lot of time directing plays, too much time in my final year. I even invited the great and the good to come to the opening nights – on one occasion I was reliably informed that the great Ken Tynan had turned up as a guest of George Steiner, though I never discovered what he thought. Perhaps mercifully. But this career path never led anywhere after university. Instead, I soon gravitated towards arts education, which I haven't regretted for a second – if anything I wish I'd become involved in art schools long before I actually did. But I still get a twinge when I see a particularly memorable, inspiring or stimulating production of a play – the thought that if the cards had fallen differently, maybe I wouldn't have been in the audience but backstage with the cast or in the auditorium taking notes.

Another minor regret is that in some photographs I tend to resemble Robert Winston, much more so than in real life. With the result that taxi-drivers and sometimes passers-by tend to say, 'You're that Winston bloke', and then they talk about fertility. At moments like that, I wish I was spending more time at the office. *Private Eye* even published pictures of the two of us, side by side, and invited readers to spot the difference. Maybe I should have on my tombstone: 'HE WAS NOT ROBERT WINSTON'.

Other regrets? I've had a few, but far too many to mention here…

David Blunkett

LABOUR MP & FORMER HOME SECRETARY

It was the February 1974 General Election. I had never stood before, so this was my first outing in what was then a rock solid Tory seat. The battle was between Labour and the Liberals for second place. In the end, we just made it. No thanks, however, to my own somewhat unorthodox canvassing.

There we were, going from house to house (many of them extremely large) in the Sheffield Hallam constituency with a cheery 'I hope you'll be voting Labour', when, as we stepped onto the driveway of one of the houses, I realised we were making a grave mistake.

It wasn't the fierce dog, it wasn't the shout of 'No communists here' that worried me; it was the soft feel under my feet. I realised before the party activist working with me, that we were on newly laid tarmac…

The door of the house opened and just as my colleague was about to say, 'We are canvassing for the…' I said, 'Terrible mistake, Conservative canvassers, sorry about that…' and hurried down the street dragging my colleague with me rather than the other way round.

It may, of course, have been the paw marks that gave me away!

Jenni Murray
BROADCASTER

I don't have many regrets as I don't see the point in wishing things had been different, but I am sorry that I was not a more dutiful daughter. I'm an only child and neglected my parents terribly as a young woman, which must have been heartbreaking for them. We lived far away for many years and denied them a lot of pleasure in their two grandchildren. I think I made up for it in the last years of their life, probably because my own children made me realise how important it is to parents to have a close relationship. I hope I wasn't too late now they're both gone.

Roger McGough
POET

A wistful haiku…

my biggest regret
is that my books weren't around
when I was at school

Gareth Southgate

MANAGER OF MIDDLESBROUGH FOOTBALL CLUB AND FORMER ENGLAND PLAYER

When asked about regrets I can immediately think of plenty of incidents and experiences that I wish hadn't happened. We all have horrible days when at the end you just want to hide under the bedcovers!

However, when I look back on those experiences, they helped me to learn and develop as a person. I think you always learn more from the failures and difficult times; experiences which make you a stronger person.

So have I made mistakes? Yes, plenty. Do I have any regrets? No!

Samden Lhatoo

CONSULTANT NEUROLOGIST, FRENCHAY HOSPITAL

A few months before I entered medical school, I went on a climbing trip to the Eastern Himalayas in the western shadows of Kanchenjunga, the third highest mountain in the world. Somewhere around 14,000 feet on the approach to base camp, we'd just finished a hard day's march when a porter came round to say that we had company. I found a strange, unkempt and barefoot figure in a harlequin orange and green shirt with a dirty woollen blanket wrapped round his waist outside the kitchen tent. He spoke in soft Bengali to explain himself. He was on a pilgrimage and wished to drink the holy waters of the glacial lakes; he was simply there and wished to make no demands of us.

With four weeks of precious rations and a load of expensive climbing gear to account for, it was explained politely but firmly to him that he would have to find another campsite. It was only minutes later when I saw him leaping from boulder to boulder up the moraine away from us that I realised he carried no sack or rucksack.

Six years later, having graduated and already exhausted myself with the physical and emotional rigours of acute hospital care, I was in the area again, hoping to recharge myself with the life-affirming frisson of the Himalayan climb. At 17,000 feet, sheltered under a large, overhanging rock, we found a pile of bones sitting on an old blanket, a tilted skull silently staring skyward. There was no mistaking the harlequin shirt, now a faded green and yellow rag, the colours long leached by years of snows and melts. There were no shoes. The Sherpas sprinkled sweets amongst the bones and murmured prayers.

It's not likely that he survived for too long after we saw him, at that altitude, clad as he had been. What consuming mental illness or deep despair had brought him so far from home? It had to be one or the other or both. Did his loved ones know where and how he passed away?

The thought of having passed the opportunity to speak to and help this otherwise apparently well man filled me with lasting regret. I'll never know if it would have made the slightest difference or if I would feel differently were I not a physician. However, I will never forget the sight of a thin, leaping, misunderstood figure in a gaudy shirt, retreating upwards from the grey moraine, and from this world.

Bette Davis
ACTRESS 1908–1989

I do not regret one professional enemy I have made. Any actor who doesn't dare to make an enemy should get out of the business.

David Jones

**FORMER CHIEF EXECUTIVE AND CHAIRMAN OF NEXT PLC
AND CO-FOUNDER OF THE CURE PARKINSON'S TRUST**

My one regret in life is that I did not buy Next and take it private in 1988 when I had the opportunity. If I had had the courage I would have made enough money to have helped to find a cure for Parkinson's Disease, which I have had for over 25 years.

☜

Uri Geller

PSYCHIC & AUTHOR

'**L**ove means never having to say you're sorry.' One of the first movies I ever took my future wife, Hanna, to see was *Love Story*, and I've used Ali McGraw's famous line many times since. It works so much better than a plain apology. John Lennon heard me say it, years later in New York, and he reduced both Hanna and me to tears of laughter by quipping, 'Love means having to say you're sorry every fifteen minutes!'

Love Story still makes us weepy and, even though that line is corny, I believe it's true. Real love is unconditional, with no ifs and buts. Forgiveness comes as part of the deal.

I try to live my whole life that way, without apology or regrets. I've always felt strongly that it's pointless to bemoan bad decisions, because the past can never be changed – whereas the future is entirely up to us. Why whinge about the one when you could be creating the other?

There have been many tragedies in my life that I would change if I possessed the power to reverse time and bend destinies as easily as I can bend a spoon. First of all, I would prevent the abortions that robbed my mother of eight children and denied me my brothers and sisters. My father forced her to sacrifice those children – and ever since my mother revealed that awful secret to me, a few years before she died, I have been acutely aware that if those children had not died, I might never have lived.

If I could, I would restore life to the Jordanian soldier I killed in battle during the Six-Day War of 1967. That, too, could prove a fatal decision – if I had not killed him, he might have killed me. Most of all, I would travel back to 1985 and prevent the miscarriage that cost Hanna and me the life of our third child, a boy we named Gadi.

These are griefs, not regrets. None of us has the power of a god, to direct our lives the way moviemakers control a film. We're not living in a fictional universe, and the events that batter us are not part of a plotline.

To have regrets, and to fret about trivial mistakes or strokes of bad luck, is worse than a waste of time. It betrays a real lack of respect for the genuine tragedies that every one of us suffers during a lifetime. It can also lead to dangerous self-pity, and a negative frame of mind that starts to make excuses for failures. Allow yourself the luxury of regrets, and you'll soon be making excuses for yourself: 'My life would be so much better, if only I'd caught that train/dated that girl/bet on that horse.'

I'll say it again – we can't change the past, but the future is ours to create. So forget about regrets, and focus on everything that's good, and all the hope that lies ahead. Because, like it or not, all the whingeing in the world will only make things worse.

It was with this attitude that I set out to a gala dinner with my son, Dan, the chairman of the Hyde Park Estate Association. Inevitably, during the course of an excellent meal, conversation turned to property prices, and I commented that I had almost bought a block of apartments overlooking the park, just after Dan was born. In 1983 I could have snapped up 14 Hyde Park Square for £900,000. Today, the six apartments are worth a combined total of around £18 million, and fetch a monthly rent of £10,000. I might almost say I regret the decision not to buy. Almost. But when I looked at my son, resplendent in his dinner jacket, holding forth with a witty speech to his gala guests, I knew there's no regret in life that's worth a damn.

Publilius Syrus

ROMAN WRITER

I often regret that I have spoken;
never that I have been silent.

Baroness James (P.D. James)

AUTHOR

One regret is that I never learnt to drive. During 1981 I lived in Dublin for the best part of a year and at that time the Irish Republic had passed a law enabling people who had not yet gained their licence to drive, with L-plates, unaccompanied. So I bought a second-hand Fiesta and started taking lessons.

Unfortunately, my instructor, who seemed rather old to be still working, had once been a bus driver in London and seemed to believe that this was also my aim. On our drives together, during which he constantly manipulated the dual controls so that I gained a somewhat optimistic impression of my competency, he kept instructing me to watch out for the next bus stop and warned me that when I was tested by London Transport, a walnut would be placed behind the rear wheel and if I crushed it when I started the engine, they would disqualify me.

This, and the tendency of Dublin drivers to regard a red light as a friendly warning, made my initiation something of an ordeal. A veil is best drawn over my humiliating failure to pass the test and I never took it again, either in Ireland or at home. Perhaps it is just as well. Even my fertile imagination cannot envisage a situation which could be improved by having me at the wheel of a car.

Tim Smit

CHIEF EXECUTIVE AND CO-FOUNDER OF THE EDEN PROJECT

My music business partner, Charlie, and I had just finished making some records with supermodels and had had enough of turning sows' ears into silk purses, when we got a call from a mutual friend to say that a girl was coming over to do a showcase at Stringfellows. She was a model whose mother was a singer and aunt was a singer, and were we interested? We plumped for an evening at home cooking pasta as we just couldn't face it. It was a real shame that the aunt was Dionne Warwick, the mother was called Cissy Houston and the daughter actually turned into quite a useful singer called Whitney! Oh well!

PRESIDENT, ROYAL MENCAP SOCIETY

Obviously I have regrets for unfulfilled dreams, but frankly, I have reached the age of 83 with few, if any, regrets about missed opportunities. I wanted to be a successful actor manager, and I was – for 30 years. I wanted to go to Mencap, first as the CEO, then as Chairman and finally as the President. I have achieved all those positions and now, in the Lords, I am able to help effect legislation for people with learning disabilities. So I can't complain, but I would have liked to be a doctor as well – and to play cricket for Yorkshire!

FORMER CRICKET UMPIRE

The one regret in my life is that I should have stayed at Yorkshire County Cricket Club, and not gone to Leicestershire County Cricket Club.

In the end it may have been the best for me, life holds so many mysteries. In any case, the rest is history, so really I have no regrets.

Michael Baum

PROFESSOR EMERITUS OF SURGERY AND VISITING PROFESSOR OF
MEDICAL HUMANITIES, UNIVERSITY COLLEGE LONDON

*A*t the end of May 2007 I celebrated my 70th birthday with a big party in the presence of 40 family members and friends over a hot weekend in the country. I watched with delight as my eight grandchildren aged between three and 10 years performed a well-rehearsed and choreographed song and dance to the words of 'We love you, Grandpa'. My wife (for more than 40 years) looked gorgeous in a party frock; many distinguished colleagues who are also close friends spoke warmly of my academic successes; we drank fine wines and a bottle of 70-year-old port and danced frenetically to the music of the Cardiff University students' big band. For the first time in my life I allowed myself to sit back and reflect complacently on my achievements and the good fortune I enjoyed with such wonderful family and friends. One deep regret, shared by us all, was the absence of my youngest brother, David, who had died just short of his 60th birthday eight years ago while holding office as President of the Royal College of Paediatrics and Child Health. However, that tragic event had been outside of my control.

I can confess, though, after a lifetime in denial, one dark secret, one missed opportunity, which has haunted me all my life. My regret concerns rugby football. I love rugby and think it's the best spectator sport of all but I didn't always want to be a spectator; I wanted to be a player. I wasn't ambitious enough to want to score the last-minute drop goal that allowed England to beat the All Blacks, or even play for the Wasps; I only wanted to play for my school's first XV. Of course I wasn't big enough to play in the pack, or fast enough to play on the wing, but I was sufficiently nimble and quick-witted to have made a useful scrum half.

So what stopped me? Well, I grew up in an orthodox Jewish household and Shabbat was devoted to the synagogue and quiet study. Saturday was also the day for rugby practice and matches of our school XV. Even if I slipped away in the afternoon on a pretext, I was so full of *cholent,* the traditional Sabbath hotpot, there was not enough blood left to flow to my legs, as most of my circulation was diverted to my gastro-intestinal tract. So I regret all that time spent in the synagogue, praying in a language I didn't understand, listening to boring sermons and eating heavy midday meals, when I could have played scrum half for the school and, who knows, even for my medical school.

But then there is a law of unintended consequences. I might have left the fold, suffered brain damage and missed out on that occasion when I met my current wife. The sliding doors of life might then have left me at 70 as a lonely, grumpy old man without a woman to call his own and without adorable grandchildren.

Bruce Oldfield

FASHION DESIGNER

Apart from the huge raft of regrets that are bound to accompany middle age, the one that I plan to address before long is to learn about music. Since a child I have loved music in all its forms but never learnt how to read it nor how to play an instrument. I'm intrigued by music's power to alter or enhance our moods; in my opinion, it's a power that no other artistic discipline can match, and I feel that it's not too late to study and better understand it on both an academic and an emotional level.

Christine Hamilton

AUTHOR AND WIFE OF FORMER POLITICIAN NEIL

I am often asked whether I regret some things that hit the headlines. For example, standing up so loudly and strongly to Martin Bell (the man in the white suit), Neil's so-called 'Independent' opponent during the 1997 election. Afterwards the press rained down on me – I was the 'wife from hell', 'bossy termagant', 'monstrous liability', and the subject of cruel and vicious cartoons.

But do I regret it? The answer is a resounding 'no' – it was one of the best things I have ever done in my life! First of all, because you should always stand up for what you believe in – in this case, my husband and the truth. Also, although I didn't realise it at the time, that confrontation put me firmly on the map in my own right, launched my career as a battleaxe and kick-started everything that has followed. Bell later said that nothing he had encountered in the Bosnian war zone had prepared him for the shock of meeting Mrs Hamilton. What a wimp!

Equally, people feel I must regret the libel action which my husband took out against a certain Mr Fayed, which resulted in Neil being forced into bankruptcy to the tune of over £2 million. Absolutely never, not at all. It was the right and only thing to do at the time and, had we not gone ahead with the court action, we would have spent the rest of our lives regretting it.

Away from the headlines, it is the same – no regrets. Regrets are a waste of time – it happened, you did it – now get on with the rest of your precious life, which flies by far too quickly to spend it worrying about the past.

Live life to the full but always make time (yes, it *is* possible to make it, however busy you think you are) for others, especially when they are in trouble. Don't worry if you miss a friend's wedding – there will probably be another one coming along later – but make all effort to go to a funeral; that really is your last chance. On your deathbed, you're not going to regret missing a holiday, a party, a business deal, but you will regret the time you didn't spend with and give to family and friends.

I certainly don't regret any of the things I've done – all part of life's rich, rewarding tapestry – but I do regret some of the things I didn't do. It's the boys I didn't kiss, not the odd fling that was a mistake! I wish I'd taken a gap year – it wasn't so easy then and the choice was more limited, but how I envy today's youngsters setting off for a year of fun, freedom and adventure before settling down to reality!

But enough of that – regrets are for yesterday, life is for now and you make your own tomorrow.

Sir Alex Ferguson

MANAGER OF MANCHESTER UNITED FOOTBALL CLUB

I think there are always moments in your life when you look back and say, 'I wish I hadn't done that or said such and such', but you should never regret the past. I certainly don't because I consider myself lucky in the life I've had.

I believe my generation were adolescents at a time of change in Britain. The war had ended, and as young teenagers growing up with that freedom and the oncoming boom of rock and roll music, Elvis Presley, Chuck Berry and Jerry Lee Lewis, we were all part of the 1960s revolution. There was still the Café Society, where we used to all meet on Sunday evenings; Coca Cola was our drug and the dance halls were teeming with aspiring Fred Astaires and Ginger Rogers. At my boys' club, Harmony Row Youth Club, the club leader, Bob Innes, had to put the lights out to encourage us to dance with the girls. The Platters were hot on the menu then, and most of my schoolfriends met their wives there and are still married to them, all with over 40 years of marriage.

I served my apprenticeship as a toolmaker and coming from a Socialist family I was deeply involved with the Trade Union and was proud when I led the Remington Rand apprentices to a national strike, not because I was a radical but because their conditions were unfair.

Yes, I can look back and say I wish I hadn't lost my temper on some occasions, or I wished I hadn't picked a particular team that lost, but it really drifts into insignificance when you consider my whole career and life. No, no, no regrets!

Baroness Susan Greenfield

NEUROSCIENTIST AND AUTHOR

I *don't* regret having done Classics at A-Level rather than Science.

Robert Crampton

JOURNALIST

My biggest regret is I've spent far too much of my life having regrets. Or rather, having the wrong attitude to regrets. For the first 15 years or so of my life, I didn't really regret anything. I just barrelled along, trying pretty much anything, oblivious to ridicule, getting some things right and some things wrong, and not worrying too much about the prospects of failure. People would have called me an extrovert and an optimist. I was, for the most part, happy.

And then adolescence struck, and with it self-consciousness, the fear of failure and, if not exactly introversion and shyness, something worse: a mistrust of change, of strangers, of the unknown. This second phase lasted a long time. Far too long – well into my early thirties, maybe longer. I was able to function, but I wasn't happy.

This period was marked by excessive regret. Regrets about almost every aspect of my life: where I was from, where I went to school, what I looked like, who I'd been out with, who I hadn't been out with, on and on and on. I was relentlessly negative, about the future, the present and, especially, the past.

At the time I would have said I analysed my regrets. But I didn't. I wallowed in them. It wasn't as if I regretted anything I could change. I just regretted the way things were, or rather the way I thought they were. And this wallowing in regret had a paralysing effect. It meant I was afraid to try anything new in case I failed, and was left with a whole load more regrets.

But then, gradually, I realised something profound: failure, and with it, regret, is the essence of life. If you're not regretting, you're not trying, you're not experimenting, you're not active, you're not fully alive. So now I try to generate new regrets, in the sense that I try as many new things as I can.

Many of these new things, of course, I'm no good at. I try to think about why that might be, and then I try to laugh about it, and then I try to forget about it, and move on and create some more regrets, which I then blot out with some more, and so on. And in this fashion, occasionally, I get a success.

COMPOSER 1866–1925

I often regret having come into this petty world; not that I hate the world. No, I love the world, I love high society and even the demimonde, since I'm a sort of demimondaine myself. But what have I come to do on this Earth, which is so earthly and so earthy? Do I have duties to perform here? Have I come here to carry out a mission – a commission? Have I been sent here to amuse myself? To enjoy myself a little? To forget the miseries of a beyond, which I no longer remember? Am I not unwelcome here? What should I say to all these questions? Thinking, almost from the moment of my arrival, that I was doing some good down here, I began to play a few musical airs which I myself had invented. All my troubles stemmed from there.

A.C. Grayling

PROFESSOR OF PHILOSOPHY & AUTHOR

Our deepest regrets most often relate to things done rather than undone, yet it is usually easier to confess to the latter than the former. So it is in my case. I regret not having tried much harder when young to master one or two other languages. I can read German, French and Italian with the aid of dictionaries; but am a poor speaker of them. I can speak a little Mandarin Chinese because I lived in China for a time and subsequently travelled there a lot; but am no reader of it. I studied the classical languages, Latin far more than Greek, and have never regretted a second of the time devoted to them, because they have been rich resources in a number of ways; but I gave only a fraction of the time, attention and endeavour to modern languages that I gave to the classical languages, and lost thereby.

It is obvious enough why I regret not trying hard to be a competent linguistic. To have access to the literatures of those tongues in the original, and to be able to converse on easy terms with native speakers of them, would be to live in additional worlds, to see with more eyes, to know things with more sides of one's brain. It would, in short, be an enlargement to be able to say and think things in these other ways, for expression shapes thought.

Perhaps it is never too late to try to master at least one of the languages one knows only imperfectly and partially. It would be an even greater matter for regret if one had this regret, and never tried to remedy it!

JOURNALIST & AUTHOR

I'm not very good at regret. I'm awfully good, even too good, at apology and I try to put things right fast, thus obviating potential regrets. But I have one serious regret – one which is utterly materialistic.

When I was a little girl, I acquired an extensive collection of all the very first *Wonder Woman* comic books. Eventually my literary taste matured so that I barely noticed and did not complain when my mother threw my comic books away. Each one cost 10 cents back then; now each is worth a hundred-thousand times more and would go a long way to paying off a mortgage.

Yet, even as I tell you this, I realise I cannot honestly regret scrapping the prototype feminist of my girlhood, not when Charles Dickens needed the space she took up on my bookshelves. You see? I'm just not very good at regret.

Maureen Lipman

ACTRESS AND AUTHOR

⸺⸺⸺ ⤜⤝ ⸺⸺⸺

I regret every time I speak out from an excess emotion, from the certain knowledge that I know best, from righteous anger or a sense of justice misplaced. Every time, yes, every time without fail (and especially when trying to make an impression). Every single time – eugh! – I regret it. And 'it', the absurd, unsubtle, unthought-out 'it', comes back to me like a kipper eaten in haste to leave a sour taste in my mouth and an anvil on my chest.

Still, it only lasts a few years, and actually, encroaching senility is sorting it out nicely. So, no, no regrets – not that I recall.

⤜⤝

Sir Arnold Wesker

PLAYWRIGHT AND AUTHOR

⸺⸺⸺ ⤜⤝ ⸺⸺⸺

*S*urely you need a slim volume of sheets to fill on the subject of 'regrets'. To begin, you would have to distinguish between those things you regret but could not possibly have done anything about because it was not within you; and those you could have done something about but failed to. For instance, it is no good my regretting not being a philosopher – I couldn't have been because

I don't possess that quality of thought. And it's no good regretting that I don't have that quality of thought. We are who we are.

Nor is it helpful to regret that my parents were too helplessly poor to have had any ambition for me. I would never have made it to university anyway; I had no head for retaining facts. I can't regret that, either. We have the heads we have.

I did, however, discover a talent for writing plays and I've worked hard and well at that talent producing in half a century a play for each year. And when there was no play I produced a volume of short stories and, latterly, a novel. It's an output of which I'm proud. But here comes my regret.

Being a playwright involves more than writing plays; it involves running a business with persistence and force; you are required to be a hustler. I was no businessman, no hustler. I had no talent for confrontation. That's my regret, I was not confrontational enough.

In the world of the arts, in that beautiful world of the beautiful arts full of beautiful souls, reside monsters: poisonous, badmouthing creatures up to whom one must stand. I was not good at it, and on the occasions I dared to stand up I did so disastrously.

Year after year I quietly wrote my plays and prose and constantly put one foot wrong after another. This, I could have done something about. I failed. And this (in addition to much else, it must be said) I regret.

Fleur Adcock

POET

*I*t's January. Forty years ago, when I first lived in this house, my garden would have been covered with snow. You don't expect me to tell you about my more private regrets, but one that weighs on me more and more heavily is that I've lived long enough to see global warming begin its relentless destruction of the world I loved.

Lord Archer

AUTHOR & FORMER CONSERVATIVE PARTY DEPUTY CHAIRMAN

Not playing cricket for England
(not good enough)

Not having a daughter
(I blame my wife)

Getting older every day
(why don't we go up to the age of 50 and then turn
round and start growing younger again?)

ASTROLOGER

I can't really say that I have had any regrets as such, as being an astrologer I believe that on the advice and direction given cosmically we can make our own choices and decisions.

But I do know I have only half accomplished my theatrical goals. This is not so much a regret as I am in control of my destiny, but recent success in plays in Brighton and Scarborough made me realise how much I missed being on stage – even more so when I read the extremely positive and praiseworthy reviews about my roles in the national press. As a result I am seeking to pick up further pieces of live performance and fulfil that part of my potential that has never fully been realised – now *that* is what astrology is all about, the realisation and fulfilment of one's gifts.

If the word regret comes into it, then I wonder if I should have continued in showbiz and kept astrology as a hobby? But I cannot turn the clock back and in the great scheme of things I have probably been offered lots of good things as a result of becoming the Astrologer Royal – so it's a case of celestial swings and terrestrial roundabouts. The plan now is to make my celebrity work for me in areas that I want to aspire to.

Andrew McEvoy

**CONSULTANT NEUROSURGEON, NATIONAL HOSPITAL
FOR NEUROLOGY AND NEUROSURGERY**

---

*T*o once have stood at five minutes to three in the tunnel at Anfield in the famous red shirt. To look at my opponents lining up. To hear 'George' introduce my name to the crowd. To hear the roof of the stadium lifted as the Kop sing 'You'll Never Walk Alone'. To move down the stairs with the clatter of studs, and touch the sign of the Liver Bird for luck, rising the last few steps to the cold air and roar, and to see the flags and banners away to my right. This is Anfield!

Ingrid Bergman

ACTRESS 1915–1982

I have no regrets, I wouldn't have lived my life the way I did if I was going to worry about what people were going to say.

Hilary Mantel

AUTHOR

*Y*ou should try to avoid the major regrets, miasmic drifts that can settle on your life and obscure the future: eschew the wistful, shut out the might-have-been. But Olwen's legs do not fall into these categories, and I think about them often.

I felt, you see, they could have been mine, for Olwen was my cousin, and it all depended on a shake of the genetic dice; it was this knowledge that distinguished my feelings about them from mere envy. I was 10, stunned speechless by life's growing terrors, fair and blue-eyed with stick limbs. Olwen was older, and solid muscle to my ghostliness. She was broad set and a glowing brown, as if she had been basted. Her face was rubbery and full, her glossy hair slicked back; her ponytail was like a twist of liquorice.

In those days I trembled with propitiatory eagerness, my eyes shining with fever and fear and anxiety to be at the life to come. Olwen, with her friends, leaned against the wall. Above her scuffed lace-ups and her ankle socks, her legs curved plumply, like the legs of a piece of furniture. A wet light shimmered along them: rounded shinbone, meaty calves. And – this is what riveted my attention – every inch of them was speckled over with black pinheads. When I was a child, a rag doll, a puppet, Olwen was a woman; she was shaving her legs.

Olwen's friends were superior to hopscotch. On rare occasions, one of them would launch herself from the wall and execute some game, skipping or hopping, seeking but never hiding, with a rapid and ferocious competence. Then, shrugging, she'd lean against the wall again, sneering at 'kids', giggling at coded jokes.

There used to be no name for the quality Olwen possessed. There is now, though, and if I ever possessed it, it was gone in the blink of an eye. I would go through my teens an anxiety-junky, inky hands trembling, tights laddered, hair tangled, heels worn down, my effort always too much for the occasion, my hopes disproportionate and my nerves in shreds. But Olwen? Olwen was cool.

Graham Norton

COMEDIAN

Moi, je ne regrette rien.

Ann Widdecombe

CONSERVATIVE MP

I regret making the mistake of thinking that once I had a skill I would always have it. As a child, I was a genuinely magnificent swimmer (easily of competitive standard) because I grew up in Singapore where leisure time was largely spent in or on the water. However, when I came back to this country in the 1950s, it was not yet the age of the municipal swimming baths and there were simply no facilities for me to keep up the hobby. When I then hit the water again, a few years later, I was disconcerted to find that my beautiful dive had turned into a rather embarrassing belly flop!

A little older, I learnt to ride a horse, but when I entered Parliament, I gave up the hobby because I did not have time. More than a decade later, I was invited back onto a horse for a television documentary and discovered I scarcely knew one end of it from the other. Certainly, I can no longer ride with either confidence or competence.

In my teens, I learnt to play the piano, but gave it up to concentrate on O Levels, and now I cannot make my right and left hands do different things on the keyboard and I certainly can no longer read music.

Then I went to university and read Latin and fondly assumed I would always be able to read Latin. After decades of neglect, my efforts to do so are now positively embarrassing.

Therefore, my advice to young people is always: 'If you have a skill, keep practising, even if only occasionally.'

ACTOR

I was once asked by a zealous interviewer if there was anything I regretted. It is a fairly frequent question and while racking my brains for an answer that I was prepared to divulge, I had a flash of inspiration and instinctively declared that I regretted everything.

A look of consternation appeared on the young man's face. 'Everything? Why?' I went on to say that the actions of one's life are made up of a series of choices governed by the information available at the time. He still looked puzzled. 'That's why I regret everything,' I explained, 'I could always have made a better choice.'

~

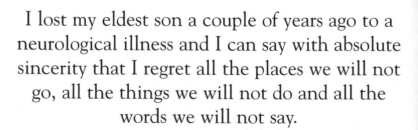

MUSIC PRODUCER

I lost my eldest son a couple of years ago to a neurological illness and I can say with absolute sincerity that I regret all the places we will not go, all the things we will not do and all the words we will not say.

Barry Cryer

COMEDIAN AND WRITER

---

1. I've never eaten a prawn sandwich without some prawns falling out.

2. I've never met Cherie Blair. I'd like to tick that one off.

3. I've never, successfully, found the end of a roll of Sellotape . If my wife's not there, I surrender.

4. I once met Margaret Thatcher and didn't have the chance to really tell her. She was already shaking hands with the next person.

5. I've never been mistaken for Brad Pitt.

6. I once watched *Deal or No Deal*. That's an hour of my life I'll never get back.

Geoffrey Palmer

ACTOR

I have two main regrets in life. The first is that I could have conned my way into going to university, which was then basically Oxford or Cambridge – not on merit but on the basis of being an ex-service man. The second is that I didn't start fishing earlier in life.

Kate Chandler

VETERINARY NEUROLOGIST, ROYAL VETERINARY COLLEGE

When I was a newly graduated veterinary surgeon, I was treating an elderly cat, Sooty, belonging to a lovely middle-aged couple. They were distraught that their cat was not eating anything and literally wasting away. Sooty was in very poor body condition and had severe dental disease. After examining the cat, I was suspicious that he wasn't eating because of his severe tooth problems. The couple had very little money but could just about afford dental treatment, and nothing else. We elected to go ahead with a thorough dental treatment under anaesthesia. I probably raised their hopes too much regarding the chances of success, but I desperately wanted to help.

Following the treatment, the cat was no better. He went home and continued not to eat. A week or so later, on further examination, I discovered that he had lumps on his kidneys which I had not detected before. He probably had cancer or chronic kidney failure, which I had failed to notice before the tooth treatment. Eventually he was put to sleep and the owners were devastated. I have regretted my approach to this case for years, because the owners trusted me to make the best decision for their cat, and in this circumstance, I failed them. Not only that, they spent all their money trying to save Sooty. I regret being too positive about this case and wish that I had discussed it with a senior colleague before the owners committed themselves to expensive treatment that was not guaranteed to cure Sooty.

Emma Tennant
AUTHOR

What I chiefly regret is my inability to regret any of the (often hasty, unthought-out and plain wrong) decisions I have made in my lifetime. These have frequently led to actions equally regrettable – but I can only look forward and so miss the divine luxury of indulging in regret.

Edith Piaf was right: regretting nothing is the only way (unless, of course, you are Adolf Hitler). So let's say the decisions and actions that have harmed only oneself need not be later regretted, for that way the swamps of nostalgia are avoided and 'the road not taken' never thought of again.

CONCERT PIANIST

A man about to turn 65 who is healthy, active, doing what he loves to do, with a marvellous wife, son and daughter, all well, and whom Life is treating kindly, has no right or reason to have regrets. It is a time for counting blessings and realising how fortunate one has been – up to now!

As a concert pianist I am privileged to envelop myself with the greatest music ever written, and to have the joy of sharing this music with my fellow music lovers through concerts, particularly concerts in which I speak briefly to the audience about the compositions they are about to hear, making their listening experience more meaningful than just a pleasant 'ear wash' of sound. Yet, few understand that an artist is constantly living with frustration and regrets – both artistically and professionally.

One definition of a musical masterpiece is that the work is better than it can be played and that no one interpretation of the composition relates all that the work has to offer – the greater the piece of music, the more this is so. One spends a lifetime studying, interpreting and performing a work such as a Beethoven Sonata and no matter how well you may play it, you always regret that which should have been better. Climbing these artistic mountains is never-ending and after a while one must get practical or go mad – you are *never* going to give the performance of the work that you have in your 'mind's ear' – one can only hope that the current performance was better than the last, and the next will be better still. Thus, everything is a 'work in progress'.

As someone who performs 85 to 90 concerts a season, one should, at my age, be thinking of cutting back, not adding more! Yet, there are so many places I would love to play, particularly in Britain, in Europe, and Japan – places where in my youth I performed often; and now concert invitations to perform in these places go not to me but to grand old masters with box-office names, or the newest, youngest, 'hottest' performer – and I am neither. Can one regret that he is not a famous master with a household name, or regret that he is no longer young and promising?

I do feel that I am playing better than I ever have, and am getting better each season – the interpretations have more to offer; my piano playing is more colourful and secure. Yet my biggest regret, and it is shared by everyone, is the realisation that age and ageing take their inevitable toll – the nervous system, the memory, the agility and strength of the hands, the ability to deal with stage fright – the diminuendo is unavoidable. When Haydn was on his deathbed, already a very old man, he apparently said, with obvious regret, 'God, how can You take me now? I am just learning how to write for the clarinet.'

William Faulkner

NOVELIST AND POET 1897–1962

Tomorrow night is nothing but one long sleepless wrestle with yesterday's omissions and regrets.

Tony Benn

FORMER LABOUR MP & CABINET MINISTER

regret that I did not always listen to my Inner Voice which invariably gave me good advice about what I should and should not do – for if I had followed that Voice I don't think I would have had many regrets to describe.

Anonymous

FORMER ROYAL MARINES COMMANDO SERVING IN IRAQ, 2003

Throughout the 18 months I spent in Iraq between 2003 and 2005, I had the responsibility (among other things) for recruiting and training Iraqi guard forces. My area of operation was rather exposed so we decided we would use the local forces, to put much-needed money into the local community and to gain some popularity, thereby giving us a little protection.

The local men were enthusiastic but totally uneducated. In fact, many of them had never worn shoes and we struggled getting them to wear the boots we supplied.

When I recruited the men I specifically asked for ex-soldiers hoping that this would give me a decent starting point. However, it soon became apparent that their skills were extremely rudimentary. I started with basic weapon drills; safe carriage, load/unload, cleaning, etc. After a few days they started to get it. I drilled them over and over until it became second nature and they began to look like decent guards. One man, who was quite a bit older than the rest – maybe 50 years old – was struggling. He was just not mentally present. While I was teaching he would be staring off into the distance and when I asked him to demonstrate a skill he would carry out the same unsafe routine he displayed on day one. As the others advanced I became increasingly frustrated. I felt that he just wasn't interested in what we were offering. He had this annoying habit of looking far off into the distance and chewing from side to side like a camel; I named him the 'camel'.

One day, I asked him to come out in front of the class and

demonstrate a 'make ready', which is cocking the rifle and putting a round into the chamber. He vacantly pointed his AK directly at me and cocked it. This is about the most dangerous thing you can do. His trigger finger was curled round the trigger, another highly dangerous practice. I knew that his magazine was empty (for training purposes), but I was so incensed that I shouted at him. I grabbed his AK and kicked him on his thigh. I immediately regretted it as he stood there looking at me in that confused way. I sat him back down with the rest and continued with the class.

At the end, when everyone else stood up to leave, the 'camel' approached me. Using my interpreter he said that he liked me and respected me but please would I not kick him again. I was totally gutted. I felt so ashamed of my lack of patience. I responded by saying that I was very sorry for kicking him. I explained that what he did was so dangerous that I lost my temper but I regretted it. I asked him to please listen to what I was teaching in future because it was important, but that I would never touch him again in that manner. Even my interpreter seemed ashamed on my behalf.

I will never forget that incident. I was teaching men who were so basic according to our own values but he had stood up to me with such quiet strength that I just stood there feeling like a schoolboy again following a gentle reprimand from a teacher. I often think about the incident and flush with shame. It is the one thing I most regret doing and I vow never again to let my feelings of being an inadequate teacher be vented as anger towards my students.

Miriam Margolyes

ACTRESS

Of course I have some regrets, despite a happy and well-filled life. They are, in the order they occur to me:

1. I should have lost weight forever when I was 22. Ridiculous to be fat all your life. I never thought I was ugly but still…

2. I wish I'd learnt Hebrew when I was 13. I am not religious but it's part of my heritage and I was lazy and let it go. I wish I'd learnt Italian and French properly, and perhaps more than anything, I wish I'd learnt Yiddish, that curious, mixed language of the European Jew. It would connect me with my past and would have enabled me to speak to the people I met in Belarus when I searched for my long-murdered family. You know, I still might learn all these languages. There is a tiny bit of time left.

3. I wish I'd bought a house in Abbey Road for £80,000, which would have made me so rich when I was still young. I didn't like the house, even though I knew it was a 'good buy'. I always buy with my heart, not my head; usually it's a good thing, but I let this one slip, alas. I pass it now and shake my fist.

4. I regret I didn't ask my older relatives about their lives and retrieved all the names and stories of the family. Now I spend hours trying to find all that out – it would have been so simple, but I didn't know then.

And that's it: no more regrets, just gratitude for a life of love and fun.

Richie Benaud

COMMENTATOR AND FORMER AUSTRALIAN CRICKET CAPTAIN

---

*N*o regrets, but there was a time when talking with Keith 'Nugget' Miller, the great Australian cricketer, that he reminded me never to discount how much luck plays a part in one's life. We were playing for New South Wales against South Australia at the Adelaide Oval in November 1950 and the South Australian captain, Phil Ridings, had given us a tremendous hammering, with South Australia making almost 400 on the opening day.

It was blisteringly hot and, at the close of play, we were sitting in the NSW players' lounge looking across the ground at St Peter's Cathedral, when Sir Donald Bradman walked past the front of the area.

'Evening everyone,' he said, 'warm out there?'

'Evening, Sir Donald,' we murmured.

Miller continued to look at the cathedral saying nothing and, being young and a bit inexperienced in only my second season, I thought I would confide something of tremendous interest to him and the rest of the team.

'Nugget,' I chirped. 'You know Bradman retired last summer and that was the same time I first played Sheffield Shield? It has always been my greatest regret I never had the chance to bowl at him.'

That caught Miller's attention and he looked at me rather than the cathedral.

'Son,' he said, 'everyone in his lifetime has one really big slice of luck. Trust me, that was yours!'

Laurence Llewelyn-Bowen

INTERIOR DESIGNER & TV PERSONALITY

Any regrets?
Have you not seen my wardrobe
from the mid-1990s?

Robert McCrum

JOURNALIST AND AUTHOR

In the summer of 1995 I spent two months in the National Hospital recovering from a stroke. During those frustrating weeks of immobilisation, I reviewed my 40-something years and argued with myself about my losses. There was, I think, some bitterness, and a lot of regrets. Now, more than 10 years on, I really can't remember what they were.

Bel Mooney

JOURNALIST AND AUTHOR

When I was younger I used to play Edith Piaf and sing along, 'Non, je ne regrette rien', sincerely believing it to be true. I liked the posture, that you would stand by all your deeds, and would say, in the words of the poet W.B. Yeats, that I 'measure the lot, forgive myself the lot.' In one way it's a good position, since you could waste your life away wondering what would have happened had you done this or not done that. Yet there is an arrogance there too, and as I grow older I feel less arrogant, more humble.

When I was asked to write something for this book I was astonished when one thing alone popped, unbidden, into my mind. Truly, I hadn't thought of it before. I found myself looking back to the end of the 1960s and wishing with all my heart that my young husband and I had gone travelling together – as so many young couples do now. Maybe we were just at the beginning of all that, yet the hippy trail was in full swing and still we did not ever once discuss throwing caution to the wind and shouldering backpacks and just going – taking a year off together, just the two of us.

Why not? Jonathan Dimbleby and I married – madly in love, and also truly excited to have met an intellectual equal – in February 1968 after knowing each other for less than four months. We were in our second year at University College London, me reading English, Jonathan reading philosophy. When we graduated in the summer of '69 we treated ourselves to a whole month camping in France and Italy, before jumping onto the bandwagon of work, work, work, which was to whirl us round for the next 35 years, until our marriage disintegrated with dramatic suddenness in 2003.

I regret not taking trains and boats and planes with him, wondering where we would fetch up. Looking at the stars from strange balconies; talking to strangers in bars and laughing about them afterwards; learning to rely on each other and feeling free.

I wish we hadn't been so serious, so faux grown-up, so influenced by relatives, so ambitious, so fixated on new mortgages and old ambition. I wish we had known then what we know now, that young couples need to focus on each other even if it means sacrificing the world. Be together, kids, I say! I regret the independence we learnt, but I will never regret that wonderful, impulsive marriage, or the love that survives its end.

Sir Cameron Mackintosh

MUSICAL IMPRESARIO

I wish I'd learnt to play the piano. Even though I was inspired to go looking for a piano in *Salad Days* when I was eight, I have always envied anyone who can just sit at a keyboard and create wonderful music. For me it is the most totally satisfying musical instrument in the world.

When I'm considering whether I want to take on a new musical, one of my tests is that the score must sound exciting even when played only on the piano. Good tunes don't need an orchestra and two grand pianos can sound like one.

Adam Mars-Jones

AUTHOR

I regret defaulting on a neurologist's bill, over 10 years ago now. One day I had experienced difficulty processing language. I was transcribing an interview I had done for the *Independent*, and my eye started noticing that my hand was badly distorting the spelling. A wave of panic hit me, and I realised that I was now writing letters that had no business in the words I was trying to shape. I made a phone call to my editor, just to see if he might detect any oddity in my way of expressing myself aloud. I seemed to pass this test, though I felt emotionally very remote, not sure what was banter in our conversation and what was straighforward. Still, it seemed that I didn't need urgent medical attention. I arranged to see my GP, and phoned a friend who lived nearby to keep me company until the time for my appointment. The friend, when she arrived, told me that I seemed normal, though uncharacteristically long-winded. This made me seem stoned. To me it felt as if my vocabulary had dwindled to about 30 words, and I was trying to convey nuances with a mind full of pebbles.

My GP said he could find nothing wrong. He suggested I might have had a transient ischaemic attack (TIA) – a mini-stroke. These things happen. Sometimes they portend worse disruption. Sometimes they don't.

For someone who makes his living processing language, a fault in the mechanism was an alarming idea. The GP gave me the name of an eminent neurologist and I went to him as a private patient. He did various tests, none of them conclusive. He suggested that I might have had an anomalous migraine with no accompanying pain (I reported a slight lateralised headache the day after the attack), but the assumption of a TIA seemed to hold good. I remember later regaining some confidence in my brain when I did an interview for the paper in French with a writer who had no English. My French wasn't brilliant, but then it never had been. My hand kept returning to my scalp, to dislodge the itchy remains of the glue that had been used to attach the electrodes for an early-morning EEG. I seemed to be fine.

When the neurologist's bill arrived, I kept putting off paying it. It was for £400 – not peanuts, but the man was eminent in his field and the money was there in my account. Logically I should have rushed to write the cheque, as a way of declaring the episode closed, but I didn't. Reminders came, but I ignored those too. The rational impulses inside the brain, after all, are massively out-numbered, and I felt a resistance that was close to superstitious. I dare say the sum was too small to justify the use of debt collectors, court orders or hitmen. But I'd better not expect to see the neurologist in question the next time my wiring goes wrong, eh?

Benjamin Disraeli

FORMER BRITISH PRIME MINISTER 1804–1881

Youth is a blunder;
manhood a struggle;
old age a regret.

Joe Mace

TV PRESENTER

Regrets: never having learnt a language or an instrument when I was young enough to have the brain space and the time to do it. Now I feel too old and my head is full of rubbish (mainly facts about football formations and the range of nappy sizes available).

Also I regret not having made my feelings known to my next-door neighbour Debbie White sooner. When I finally plucked up the courage to ask her out, she announced she and her family were moving house the next day. My first broken heart.

Arabella Weir

COMEDIAN AND WRITER

No regrets – it's best not to allow yourself any regrets; they only serve to make you think you could have been a 'better' person if only you'd tried harder. People who always did the right thing and have no regrets aren't usually very interesting people. My regrets exist only in human form – practically everybody I've ever slept with!

Sir Philip Otton

FORMER LORD JUSTICE OF APPEAL

I have one profound and irradicable regret. My parents made considerable sacrifices, both financial and emotional, to help me to be called to the Bar. As an only child from a very modest background I was undoubtedly spoilt. Whatever I have achieved has been entirely due to the opportunity they gave me. And yet, while they were still alive I never thanked them individually or together for all they did for me. I look back with deep regret that I never once embraced them, or touched them or even whispered to them to show my affection and appreciation. Now they are gone and I never shall.

Simon Shorvon

PROFESSOR OF NEUROLOGY, INSTITUTE OF NEUROLOGY

D-503 lives in the One State, a totalitarian country, within a shiny glass edifice, that is organised on mathematical principles, and like all others, he has been programmed to act in ways prescribed by the all-powerful ruler, the 'Great Benefactor'. All life's functions are carefully controlled; food and sex are parcelled out, with each citizen receiving food and a fixed number of sexual partners based on a system of coupons and scheduling. But then D-503 falls in love (horrors) with I-330, a woman who is a member of a terrorist group that aims to overthrow the State and return society to one in which free will and imagination exist once more. The revolt is put down and D-503 is eventually captured. The Great Operation is carried out upon him – a neurosurgical procedure in which his brain is reprogrammed by the obliteration of a vital part (a splinter) of neural tissue. He then lapses back into a happy, mind-numbed robotic existence. He becomes again a digit of production in the One State factory, eating and screwing by coupon, and yet being also devoured and screwed. (*With apologies and regrets to Yevgeny Zamyatin for scrambling the words and meaning of his great 1921 novel* We.)

My choice of a favoured regret is not a personal one (these are, on the whole, uninteresting), but a more universal regret on behalf of D-503s: the regret that freedom of thought is now so often subjugated by totalitarianism and tyranny.

Regret the universal characteristics of tyrannies and tyrants!: their belief that the duties of one group are more important than the rights of another; their fear that their power will be corroded by free thought; the egotism of leadership where self-belief becomes delusion; the aesthetic of violence and efficiency; their narcissistic self-regard. D-503s beware the ruler who ceases to think of himself as your servant, whose self-righteousness overcomes self-doubt, who considers opposition as 'threatening society', and whose actions become inevitably rooted in self-interest (in One State, the Great Benefactor is the only person allowed to exercise free will – and does so almost entirely to maintain his own position). That power always corrupts is a general rule; there are few exceptions.

The 'Great Operation' was a triple irradiation of a pathetic brain node in the region of the pons Varolii. It had the immediate effect of removing fantasy. This rings bells to me as a neurologist, daily encountering patients suffering from degenerations of the brain which result in a reduction of personal freedom, dissolution of the personality, reduction in dissent and in imagination, loss of control, and diminished humanity. The great operation, these diseases and tyrannies, as Zamyatin implies, are all common enemies of free will; and envisage how modern totalitarian states would no doubt embrace such neurosurgical technology if such a brain node could be located. As in disease, so too in One State, imagination is removed, and, *note bene*, with it regret, which requires imagination for sustenance. One thing is clear – we should fear the absence of regret.

Sue MacGregor

JOURNALIST & BROADCASTER

To give you personal regrets would take too much time. There are so many and it would be too boring! Here's a quote I like from Samuel Johnson, in 1750:

'Let us… make haste to do what we shall certainly at last wish to have done; let us return the caresses of our friends, and endeavour by mutual endearments to heighten that tenderness which is the balm of life.'

Timothy Bavin

BENEDICTINE MONK OF MELTON ABBEY; FORMERLY
BISHOP OF JOHANNESBURG, THEN PORTSMOUTH

T hat Chopin had written a sonata for cello and piano came as a surprise to me when I heard it recently on the radio. I wasn't particularly struck by it, but I was reminded again of a missed opportunity and the regret which I feel at not having learnt to play the cello.

I had the chance of doing so as part of a choral exhibition that took me from Windsor to Brighton College, and which entitled me to a free musical education. However, with a schoolboy's delusion of grandeur, I set my sights on learning the organ: what noise, what power, what gadgetry, what control…

So I became a not-very-good organist (having never really mastered the piano), but missed out on an instrument which reflects very obviously the personality of its player, and for which such marvellous music has been written by Brahms, Elgar, Tchaikovsky, Finzi and Dvořák, among many others. Expensive and versatile, rich and sonorous, the cello is equally wonderful in solo and orchestral playing, but supreme in chamber music.

Alas, it's too late now and even if I were not too old to learn it, there is surprisingly little time for such study in a monastery. So I must take my regret with me to the grave – but I would like to have learnt the cello sufficiently well to be able to play Max Bruch's 'Kol Nidrei'.

Jeremy Bowen

JOURNALIST & BROADCASTER

I honestly don't have any serious regrets! I try not to have any, because there's no point. Maybe I should have gone into buy-to-let property or something, but that is about it. And I should have done more sit-ups when I was in my twenties.

C.S. Lewis

AUTHOR 1898–1963

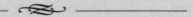

Has this world been so kind to you that you should leave with regret? There are better things ahead than any we leave behind.

Hunter Davies

AUTHOR & JOURNALIST

Oh, if only I had not been so silly and gone through my working, writing, interviewing life not using a tape recorder.

The original reason was pretty potty. It was in 1964 and I'd been sent by the *Sunday Times* to interview WH Auden. He was staying at Stephen Spender's house in St John's Wood. I had to take him an envelope from the Literary Editor. It was unsealed, so I looked inside and saw £30. Auden grabbed it, as soon as I arrived, and then seemed to lose interest in the interview, going all bored and grumpy.

It was going to be my first-ever interview with a Famous Person, so I'd borrowed a tape recorder, a Grundig, about the size of a house. I'd never used one before and was obsessed by whether it was working or not.

The interview never appeared. Possibly because Auden couldn't be arsed to answer the questions, or I was too young and nervous to ask anything decent. But I blamed the tape recorder and never used one again.

Even now, I don't use one. My rationale is that a tape recorder doubles your time. You have to listen to it all again, and half of what most people say is not worth listening to, then get it transcribed. Instead, I've always written stuff in a little notepad, editing as I go, and only writing down what I think I'm going to use. Makes it so much quicker.

But looking back, I do regret one occasion when I should have used a tape. This was when I spent 18 months with the Beatles in 1966–8, writing their only ever authorised biography.

I spent hours with them in private, in their homes, in Abbey Road. Two of them are now dead, and so are many of the other characters in the Beatles saga, such as Brian Epstein and their parents, all of whom I interviewed. Oh, if only I had thought ahead. I've got my notebooks, but even I can't read my handwriting.

Around 10 or so handwritten lyrics by the Beatles that I collected at the time, saving them from being burnt by the cleaners, are now in the British Library manuscript room, next to the Magna Carta, Shakespeare, Beethoven and Wordsworth. But how much richer a record I could have passed on if only I hadn't been so silly and refused to use a tape recorder…

ACTOR

M y biggest regret would have to be not cashing in on the success of *Chariots of Fire* and trying to make it BIG in America. At that time the pond was a little smaller than now and an English actor was offered more than just the token baddie. I absolutely love Los Angeles and would give my eye teeth and receding gums to live there now – the climate is perfect and the lifestyle is laid back and relaxed – but at the time I had a family and a new home and it all seemed too risky. I suppose things haven't worked out too badly, but there are days when I wake up and think, 'Why the hell don't I become a market gardener?' Why indeed… where did I put those free seed packets that fell out of the newspaper?

JOURNALIST AND BROADCASTER

Looking back on life after passing three score years and ten, I regret that I did not have the chance to go to university when I was mature enough to get the most out of it.

ACTOR AND AUTHOR

As Robert Brewster Beattie says in his poem 'A Way to a Happy New Year',

> 'To leave the old with a burst of song,
> To recall the right and forgive the wrong;
> To forget the thing that binds you fast
> To the vain regrets of the year that's past.'

I have six children, five boys and a girl. Apart from the first and the last, they are all teenagers. If you have teenage children, you know what that means. Mine are, without exception, computer freaks. To walk into their Computer Room is like visiting the Holy Grail. They would kill for their daily fix. On the pretext of doing homework, they play a game where they run around massacring every living thing in their path. One of them laughs *mit Schadenfreud* every time he blows somebody up! The only real rows we have in the house are about whose turn it is to kill!

Apart from this, Therese and I have got used to the idea that they prefer the company of their monosyllabic friends to the company of highly literate 'been there, done that' parents. They never see us as a source of advice, only money. They keep me awake at night and shout me awake in the morning! They never laugh at my jokes.

And I love them! Oh, how I love their little cotton socks! Having my wife and children, my family, is the best thing that ever happened to me! I was present at the birth of all six children – six miraculous moments that were also moments of revelation! You want to see a grown man cry? Have a baby!

Anyway, it was at the birth of my first, Catherine, that I saw the light. I had never seen anything like it in my life! And I was so moved that I had to find some words to express it. And this is what I said: *'When a baby is born, everything that comes before is justified.'*

That just about puts the stopper on it. A regret implies a wish to change the deed or the word, to remedy the vain regret. But that would change the past and I might never have met my wife and had six computer nuts!

I mean, just imagine – I could regret that I never invited Darcey Bussell to dinner! My dream woman! Maybe because my nose goes down and hers goes up. The yin and the yang! She would certainly have refused me, but if she hadn't, I might have married *her*! Except that Therese was also a classical dancer, she danced at Covent Garden, and she is still the most beautiful woman I know. Regrets? Pfui!

Alan Hansen

**FOOTBALL COMMENTATOR
AND FORMER LIVERPOOL & SCOTLAND FOOTBALL PLAYER**

My regret is that I never learnt to play the piano. My mother was very musical and the people I admire most are the singer-songwriters who are excellent on the piano.

Baroness Julia Neuberger

RABBI, HEALTH CAMPAIGNER & GOVERNMENT ADVISOR

I really wish that I had done some more science at school. I work so much with health professionals and have learnt a great deal from them, but some basic science would have speeded it up and made life simpler – what a shame it wasn't compulsory!

Yogi Amin

CONSULTANT NEUROANAESTHETIST,
NATIONAL HOSPITAL FOR NEUROLOGY AND NEUROSURGERY

Sinatra sang: 'Regrets, I've had a few. But then again, too few to mention.' Well that's not entirely true for me! I have many regrets: not expressing my feelings enough, not taking enough risks, especially in matters of the heart! Not always speaking up, or having opinions but not always acting on them, and perhaps being a tad too apathetic about the world around me. Not continuing to play Rugby Fives (I am absolutely convinced I would've been world champion by now – I mean, I was the school captain after all!).

Are these regrets or just lessons in life! Today, as D.H. Lawrence said, 'I want to live my life so that my nights are not full of regrets.'

Lord Stevens

FORMER COMMISSIONER OF THE METROPOLITAN POLICE

*D*uring the course of a 43-year career in the police service I have had many regrets! A big one being the fact that maybe I have not pursued as efficiently and vigorously as I would have liked investigations into offences such as murder and the like. Some people have called me a perfectionist but I suppose, in truth, it is more about never being satisfied with the effort I gave in cases where people had severe personal loss. Victims suffer from the loss of loved ones, relatives or acquaintances for the rest of their lives. As a career detective for 23 years of my police service, I saw many of these people. No matter how thoroughly you investigate horrendous crimes or how much time you spend consoling the victims' relatives, in my view it is never enough.

However, one of the biggest regrets I have is to do with when I supervised and led the Stevens One Investigative Team in Northern Ireland, which started in September 1989. I took a team over there to investigate alleged collusion between the security services and the Protestant paramilitaries. The team consisted of the best people I had worked with over 27 years and came from four different Forces. There were four heads of County CID and a number of people from the Flying Squad and Anti-Terrorist Squad at Scotland Yard. What I failed to realise, over two years of intense investigation and living in very confined accommodation in Belfast, was the toll it had taken on the 28 officers. At the end of two years we finished Stevens One and returned to the mainland. Unfortunately, I had not realised that all of them had been affected by the intensity of their work and the stress that work had inflicted on them, let alone their absence from their families over this period. All of them were affected in some way or another. Some had simulated heart attacks in the street and were taken to hospital for treatment, others had boils appearing all over their body, and four never returned to British policing and retired.

I had failed to understand that the macho culture and the approach of never admitting you were under stress had not enabled me, as the leader of the group, to understand the suffering that my team was going through. It was a lesson of a lifetime to realise that people can be under extreme stress and not show that they are suffering. So my great regret is that I did not see them individually, understand what difficulties they had and take the appropriate action to minimise and reduce the stress they were under. I have never made that mistake again and always bear in mind that different people have different levels of stress.

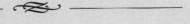

Ogden Nash

POET 1902–1971

The bed is a bundle of paradoxes: we go to it with reluctance, yet we quit it with regret; we make up our minds every night to leave it early, but we make up our bodies every morning to keep it late.

Ray Tallis

EMERITUS PROFESSOR OF GERIATRIC MEDICINE, AUTHOR AND PHILOSOPHER

———————— ~ ————————

Regret is a state of mind, as is its absence, and neither seem to have a clear causal relationship to the autobiographical facts. There are times (eg, 3am) when I am preoccupied by so many sins of omission and commission that they seem to comprise the story of my life; and there are times (eg, early evening in the pub) when the inner Piaf is in the ascendant. Then I look ahead with unfounded optimism and look back with equally unfounded satisfaction.

When I am in regret mode, I do a hurried gallop round a random selection of the things that I am sorry to have done or not done, and (most often) I wish that I had been kinder, more generous-spirited, more competent, more productive, more considerate, etc. This then prompts a second-order regret that there isn't time to make amends. A third-order regret then follows, that I have a life of finite duration, in which each action therefore has 'opportunity cost' attached to it: doing X stops me from doing Y, and so on. At this stage, I touch bedrock and resolve to squander as little time as possible in regretting things that I cannot change and as much time as possible ensuring that I will so order my affairs in future as to lay down the seeds for as little additional regret as possible. A fourth-order regret is that this resolve never works.

Meera Syal
ACTRESS AND AUTHOR

I really don't have any regrets! I think everything that's happened, good and bad, I've learnt from, laughed at or used as comedy material.

≋

Alan Titchmarsh
GARDENER, BROADCASTER AND AUTHOR

My regrets are always of omission, rather than commission; things I didn't do, rather than risks taken. When I was 17, I saw a convertible Austin Chummy for sale for £25. I dithered, and by the time I got my dad there it had gone. And I never did get one! Oh, how I pine for that Austin Chummy!

≋

AUTHOR

I wish I had taken music more seriously when I was young. As a teenager, I wrote songs and played the guitar – and I know in my heart that I had very little talent, but I still regret that the making of music isn't a bigger part of my life because it always gave me so much pleasure.

At infant school, we were given little music books for a radio programme called *Time and Tune*. Armed with these little books, and with just a toy piano (one octave, with no sharps or flats) and a small xylophone (similarly limited), I used to sit on the stairs of our small council house, aged six or seven, trying to work out for myself the mystery of the notes, and writing my own little tunes. I sometimes think – not without bitterness – that my parents, grandmother, and older sister (as they stepped over me on the way to the lavatory) might have drawn useful conclusions about getting me some music lessons, but unfortunately nobody's mind worked that way.

A few years ago, I met a chap who practised phrenology as a hobby (the 19th-century 'science' of analysing the bumps on your head). He was giving a demonstration at a Christmas fair in New York, and it's true that he just happened to sell pianos for a living. Anyway, when he was reading my head, a friend of mine asked him, 'Can you feel that she's creative?' and he replied (not completely convinced), 'Yes, mmm. I think she's maybe a musician?' My friend harrumphed a bit, thinking this was just a badly disguised sales pitch for a Bechstein, but I didn't allow her to correct him. I was all too intrigued by the answer.

J. Paul Getty

INDUSTRIALIST 1892–1976

I hate to be a failure. I hate
and regret the failure of my
marriages. I would gladly give
all my millions for just one
lasting marital success.

William Harkness

CONSULTANT PAEDIATRIC NEUROSURGEON, GREAT ORMOND STREET HOSPITAL

Yeti Airlines flight 110 drops down through the mid-morning haze, entering a long deep valley of muted browns and patches of deep green. Looking over the pilot's shoulder, through the cracked and slightly smeared windscreen of the twin propeller light aircraft, the airstrip at Lukla comes into view through the light cloud. From first impressions, the Lukla airstrip seems to be living up to expectation, being set precipitously on the side of a mountain, pitched at a steep angle and ending, somewhat disconcertingly, in a wall of rock.

The small settlement of Lukla, with its vital airstrip, acts as the gateway to the Khumbu region and thence to Everest, which explains its strategic significance. As our plane hurriedly reloads and sets off back to Kathmandu, we meet our team of porters who are introduced by Karma, our *sirdar* or guide.

Our first day's walk is to be relatively gentle, through green pastures studded with fruit trees in full blossom, a riot of pinks and reds. The paths are well worn and at frequent intervals we pass the highly decorated prayer stones marking our way towards Everest. This is the start of our 10-day adventure in the Khumbu, which is to take us above 5000 metres and into thin air.

So how did a 50-odd-year-old neurosurgeon end up with a party of friends, walking towards Everest? This particular journey began a few years ago, when I operated on a teenager whose life was being blighted by his epilepsy. In 1991 I was appointed as a consultant surgeon at the National Hospital, Queen Square, and Great

Ormond Street Hospital with a specialist interest in epilepsy surgery. I spent a six-month sabbatical in the United States, where I observed a number of both adult and paediatric epilepsy surgery programmes, and on return to the UK joined two excellent multi-disciplinary teams of experts in the field. I have now been privileged to operate on over a thousand patients with epilepsy and I can only say that the results are immensely rewarding. This particular young man had problematic teenage years as a result of his uncontrolled epilepsy and the surgery transformed not only his life but also those of his whole family. The response of this family was to organise a charity event in the form of a trek in Nepal. This generous act has now led to two charity treks to Nepal and one to Africa to raise money for the National Hospital Development Foundation and also for the National Centre for Young People with Epilepsy. The amount of money raised has been staggering and joining them on the first trek has left me with a taste of the Himalayas, which I just don't seem to be able to get rid of.

Who are my fellow trekkers? Most importantly, I am joined on this trek by my 21-year-old son, currently studying creative writing at university. We have trekked together before and he shares my enthusiasm for the beauty of the Nepalese countryside and people. Then there are my oldest and dearest friend and his son. A delightful man, also a surgeon, and sometimes known for his short fuse, he immediately relaxes within the mountain environment and gradually begins to resemble again the boy I met over 35 years ago. Also in the team are a solicitor whom I met on the first trek, and a colleague of many years who is without doubt 'the best damned anaesthetist that ever passed gas', and who becomes our self-elected expert on altitude sickness.

After the first day's gentle walking through lush valleys and through pretty villages, we start the long and punishing climb up to

Namche bazaar and our first views of Everest. Then, after a couple of days of acclimatisation in Namche, we set off towards our high-altitude goal. We are heading to Dingboche, which lies two days from base camp and will be the closest we get to Everest. On the way, the weather is variable, with some moments of snow and strong winds and others of clear blue skies and dramatic panoramas. Several of the other mountains in the range are much more dramatic than Everest, but Everest carries a mystery all of its own, characterised by the plume of snow constantly being blown from the summit and the legends of climbers past and present. It is almost impossible to put into words the spectacular beauty of the snow-clad peaks surrounding the valleys in which the trekking paths lie. At every minute of the day there is a change in the depth and texture of the light, which brings the mountains alive, with dawn and sunset becoming natural spectacles of incomparable beauty.

Our high-altitude summit is a peak above Dingboche of approximately 5300 metres and to reach it we walk upwards to where the landscape changes with gradual but brutal severity. The greenery and blossoms are replaced by rocky morrain, which leads the eye continuously upwards to the surrounding peaks. We pass through small communities, see schools where children have to walk many miles to class and visit small temples where oil lamps burn and prayer wheels turn in continuous devotion. We visit Kunde, Pheriche, Pengboche and Tengboche whose exotic names conjure up memories of other travellers and their tales and experiences. At night we talk, read, play cards, write diaries and generally catch up with all those things that life normally does not allow.

Finally though, we are ready to set off for our final challenge. We have to leave the sleepy village well before daylight, but sadly two of our party are affected by altitude sickness brought on by ill health. It is, therefore, a party of four who set out to the summit through the light snow and who witness dawn breaking over the mountains surrounding Everest and celebrate by the small chorten, which is surrounded by prayer flags. Hilary and Tenzing we may not have been, but this sort of achievement surely can have no regret.

And so, regrets? When we think of regrets it is easy to recall moments when a decision made led to an unexpected or unfavourable outcome, but these are rarely of sufficient significance to have a negative impact on one's life. Indeed, it can be the challenges of such events that are life-forming and guide us to meet future challenges. Lifelong regrets could possibly be that musical instrument you never learnt to play; but then high up in the Himalayas, it is silence and stillness one craves, not the guitar or the iPod. What of the sporting hero you might have been? A surgical career put paid to any aspirations I had of being a scratch golfer, although there is always the Seniors circuit! More seriously, these moments in the mountains are ones I would love to have shared with other family members and I hope that the future will give us that opportunity. For those family members now long gone, I hope that they can look down from above and see where life has taken me. There were many questions I never asked and many goodbyes we never had the chance of saying but that merely adds to my resolve to live life to the full with friends and family.

The route out of the Khumbu takes us back again to Lukla, where the weather is clear and somewhat disappointingly our flight back to Kathmandu will depart on time. As we rapidly gain altitude, the small windows in the cabin hold faces desperate to catch a last glimpse of the nirvana they are leaving behind, forlornly anticipating their return to the 'real world'.

Regrets? None! I shall be back!

Kate Thornton

TV PRESENTER

I regret and rue the day I started smoking above and beyond anything else I've done in my life. It's arguably the single most unintelligent decision I ever made and one I am now desperately trying to put right by quitting. I've always prided myself on my independence and can't believe I've allowed myself to become so dependent on something that is so stupidly bad for you.

Gary Lineker

SPORTS PRESENTER AND FORMER ENGLAND FOOTBALL CAPTAIN

I regret trying to chip the goalkeeper from the penalty spot against Brazil in 1992. I needed just one goal to equal Bobby Charlton's goal-scoring record of 49 for England. I was trying to be clever and I fluffed it! The keeper saved the shot and I never did equal Bobby's record. However, his goals were always so much better than mine that he deserves his record.

Sir Martin Gilbert

HISTORIAN & AUTHOR

*H*aving been fortunate in my life as a historian, writing the books I wanted to write and lecturing about my work to audiences worldwide, I have no regrets about the past. But on three occasions, each long ago, I missed opportunities that make me smile as I imagine what they might have led to. The first was in 1959, the second in 1962 and the third in 1972.

In 1959 I went to Poland on an Oxford University student exchange. The first stop was the Poznan Trade Fair. One stall was the display of a Polish pickle manufacturer, hoping to find an export outlet for his wares. How I laughed at the idea of Polish pickled cucumbers finding a British or an American market. Not for me a modest contribution to the Polish export drive.

In 1962, during a prolonged trip through the United States, I reached the desert city of Phoenix. I marvelled at the beauty of the desert landscape of cactus and scrub. On the far outskirts of the town, land was being offered for sale at $50 an acre. I had just received twice that amount as an advance for my first book. How I laughed at the idea of buying such a remote and dusty plot of land for all my earnings. Today, such an acre commands $1 million at the least.

Ten years later, in 1972, I was at a dinner with businessmen who knew a thing or two about the retail food trade. Among the guests was a man who was singing the praises of California wines and offering investment opportunities. I had just been appointed Churchill biographer and had some cash in hand. How I laughed at the idea of wine from California being able to compete with the wines of France or Italy in the British market.

Do I have any regrets? Of course not – until I go into my local Waitrose and see those Polish pickles and California wines, or I travel to Phoenix (as I did recently) and marvel at the building boom.

Claire Rayner

AGONY AUNT AND AUTHOR

I can tell you very quickly what I most regret – and that was that I didn't work harder at Latin or French when I was at school. I picked up a smattering of German but I don't particularly care about that; I'd so much like to have better French at my command! I doubt that going to classes now would do me any good – at 76 I am just about ready to turn my toes up and having French and Latin would be no use to me then. But oh, I do wish I had; I am sure that I would have been a better writer than I turned out to be with the discipline of Latin behind me.

Sir Roger Moore

ACTOR

I was discussing this regret idea with my assistant, Gareth Owen, at Pinewood Studios, and having asked him how to approach the subject he said, 'Regret? Yes, you regret not having had the letter before so that you would have had more time to think about it.'

My regrets are all far too personal for me to commit them to paper or to the ears of anyone who is not a trained and highly qualified psychiatrist.

Maeve Binchy

NOVELIST

*I*t's quite true about not regretting what you *have* done. I have no regret at all about years of being loud and wrong, and of leaving perfectly good, safe jobs for something more adventurous. I don't even regret all those foolish fallings-in-love with entirely the 'wrong people' since they sort of prepared me to realise when the 'right' person turned up.

What I *do* regret, however, is not realising that when you get to your sixties it's not as easy to learn things as it once was.

Why didn't I learn bridge when I had a bright young mind that remembered things? That way I would have known what to call when someone said something unexpected. Why did I have to wait until I was 50 and a bag of nerves to learn to drive a car, instead of crashing through the gears when I was 18 and fearless?

I always thought I would understand everything and master most things. If I had met Einstein on a good day we could have sorted relativity out together. It might have been so once but not any longer. Now my heart sinks when I see the pages of instructions with any gadget I buy .

I feel sure that if I had only got into the habit of translating centigrade into fahrenheit and pounds into kilos everything would have been done much more speedily and certainly more easily than it is now.

Brian Patten

POET

Having no regrets is regret enough

My one regret is that I have none

I have had too many regrets to
bother regretting any of them.

Philip Patsalos

PROFESSOR OF CLINICAL PHARMACOLOGY, INSTITUTE OF NEUROLOGY AND THE NATIONAL SOCIETY FOR EPILEPSY

The 7 July 2005 was a most regrettable day. I had planned to take the day off and spend it with my wife; to lie in, to relax, to have lunch and generally spend some time together, a scarce commodity in our busy lives. Instead I agreed to a 9.00am meeting that day and took the London Underground's Piccadilly Line westbound to Russell Square and a two-minute walk to my place of employment at the Institute of Neurology.

I caught the train at 8.15am, 30 minutes later than my usual time, and was pleased to sit in my favourite seat on the front carriage. The train slowly made its way, stopping regularly due to 'electrical problems' on the line. At King's Cross, as was usual, many passengers disembarked and even more passengers squeezed into the carriage. It was my cue: I was five minutes from Russell Square and as the train sped out of King's Cross, I put away my reading material and closed my briefcase, which lay across my lap. I looked at my watch; it was 8.47am and I would be in good time for my meeting.

Moments later I opened my eyes to darkness, to utter carnage and devastation. Bodies were lying everywhere, people were groaning and people were crying. It took an hour for me to be evacuated from the tunnel and a further hour to be taken by ambulance to the Royal London Hospital, where the medical staff worked hard to save my life and to minimise my severe injuries. I was discharged nine weeks and two days later, and after many months of rehabilitation and physiotherapy I continue to face many challenges. Life is no longer straightforward. The 7 July 2005 was a most regrettable day.

Michael Brearley

PSYCHOANALYST AND FORMER ENGLAND CRICKET CAPTAIN

There are big regrets in life and little ones. But the little regrets may still play on one's mind. Here's one of mine, from my cricket life.

In 1976, I was selected to tour India. In the early matches of the tour I was in the best form of my life. I liked the country, I liked the pitches, and the type of bowling appealed to me, by which I mean that I knew I could play the spinners well, and loved that particular challenge.

The first test was at Delhi. We won the toss and batted first on an excellent batting pitch. India had one medium-fast bowler, Karsan Ghavri; a medium pacer, Mohinder Amarnath; and three excellent spinners: Bishen Singh Bedi, B.S. Chandrasekar, and S. Venkataraghavan. I opened with Dennis Amiss. The noise of the crowd seemed distant, almost unreal. There were the remains of early morning mist or haze: a milky sunlight. I'd scored five, after a few overs. No alarms, one over from Bedi, to change the pacemen's ends. A beautiful butterfly settled in the batting crease. I pushed a ball from Ghavri towards mid-off and called for a single. Brijesh Patel, the quickest Indian fielder, ran from extra cover, picked up and hit one stump with his under-arm throw. I was out by a yard.

I didn't bat again in the match (which we won by an innings). Tony Greig, who was the captain of the MCC on that tour, told me he nearly cried when I ran myself out. I still nearly cry, to think of it. I regret taking that single. I still try to undo it, find myself thinking about the idiocy of the call. I failed in the next test, so a month later I had lost the prime form that I was in at that moment of opportunity at Delhi. In the third test I was caught and bowled off short leg's head for 59. If helmets had been the vogue I wouldn't have been out.

Regrets are often not only about the fact of what we did; they are often too about the motives, the character failings that led to the mistaken or foolish decision. And I know that one element in my decision to take the suicidal run was that I was uncertain about whether or not to hook Ghavri's short ball, whenever he next bowled it to me. It's not that I was scared; I'd faced Michael Holding and Andy Roberts earlier that year without flinching, and they were yards faster than Ghavri. But what a weakness! To bolt from my end because of that insecurity! And what an impact it may have had on my entire test batting career. Who knows?

Napoleon Bonaparte

EMPEROR OF THE FRENCH, (1804–15) 1769–1821

The only conquests that are permanent and leave no regrets are our conquests over ourselves.

Esther Rantzen

TV PRESENTER AND FOUNDER AND CHAIR OF CHILDLINE

Like the glorious French singer Edith Piaf, I have no regrets. Partly this is due to my very bad memory for unpleasant experiences – you could call it a psychological blocking mechanism; I call it blissful forgetfulness. Partly it's because I tend to look forward, rather than back. Mainly it's because the times I've tried and failed, the moments I've fallen over or had a custard pie thrown in my face, have all been valuable learning experiences, and I think we learn far more effectively from our mistakes than from our triumphs.

Sometimes at three in the morning I wake and find myself thinking, 'If only… I wish I had known… Why on earth did I, or didn't I?' But by the time the sun rises, and a new day begins, the regrets have flown.

POET

*M*y father died when I was 25. I regret that I didn't ask him more about his family and his life. And I wish I'd read more of his favourite books while he was alive, so we could have talked about them.

JOURNALIST & AUTHOR

I regret not running away with my neighbour's wife. This was 20 years ago. She was tall, blonde, Dutch and lived three doors down. I was unhappily shacked up with a German girl-friend – a relationship I had charged into after the collapse of my first marriage. I didn't get on with the German girlfriend but I got along with my neighbour's wife, the Dutch blonde. She was funny, smart, kind – we laughed a lot of the time. Then one night – oh, but you can guess – there was a trip to the West End to see a film preview, then a glorious snog-fest suddenly erupted under the arrow of Eros. Bed the next day, and love soon after – we just clicked.

But I was still badly bruised from the divorce court and wanted to be sure. Big mistake. She told her husband about us. Another big mistake. I think she was already looking for a way out of her marriage (I wasn't the first, although her hubby thought I was) and I was wary of this need of hers to escape. I thought I was just a convenient exit door. It collapsed, and everyone was hurt – her, me, German girlfriend, Dutch hubby (he still blames me for his marriage failure – he should blame the first guy, who is one of the biggest names in the British film industry). With the benefit of hindsight, I should have gone for it – said '*Auf Wiedersehen*, pet' to the German girlfriend and tried to make a go of it with my neighbour's wife. She was a 10, and I felt enough for her to try to make it work – even if I was panicked by her urgency and need for speed. It all ended up fine, because she met someone else and so did I; I have been married to my beautiful Japanese wife for almost 15 years and we have a four-year-old daughter who lights up my world. But I regret not giving it a go with my neighbour's wife, because she was worth it. Most relationships do not end too soon; most relationships go on far too long – but that one hardly left the launch pad, and I have to say that I regret not giving it a chance.

Steve Harley

SINGER AND SONGWRITER

My daughter, Greta, taught me not to be afraid of handling cats. She showed me how to pick up Frankie and how to wrap my right hand under his bottom, cradling his curled body into my right-angled elbow and palm grip. She'd done it all her young life. Brought up in the countryside with land and pets, it came naturally to her. She wasn't from a flat in Deptford, where even a budgie was animal *non grata*. Her brother, Kerr, said, 'Look, it's Dad's first pet.' That was in 2005 and I wished then that I had learnt to relax in the company of felines long, long ago. It felt like I'd passed a test; it was as though I'd achieved a long-held goal. I had held a cat for the first time. No regrets. Just satisfaction.

I had never ridden a bike until my neighbour Nick told me over a Guinness in the Red Lion that he had a tandem and he believed I could take the back seat, with him as pilot, and pedal around the lanes of south Suffolk. We did it first one Bank Holiday. It was a thrilling experience; at the age of 45, I was doing something so basic to the great majority, just cycling, simply pedalling, but which to me was a great achievement. Regret not having enjoyed it earlier? No. Time and place. Fate was at work.

Polio struck at my right leg in the epidemic of the early 1950s. And so I've never ridden a horse. I've owned several thoroughbreds who raced. I've been an annual member at Newmarket for 30 years, and been to several hundred race meetings. I adore the equine: John Francome coming to the last on Sea Pigeon in the Champion Hurdle, and actually taking a pull before unleashing a little rein and finally galvanising his mount to the most casual of great successes. This lives bold and bright in the memory 25 years on, and I want to feel what he felt at that moment, the moment of ultimate sporting knowledge, the moment when a pro sportsman glances about him in the heat of battle, competing at nothing less than the highest level, and affords himself a slight snigger in consideration of the ease with which the Cup will shortly be his.

Now I can ride tandem, through the jungles of Cambodia and the dunes of Death Valley, as well as along the country lanes of east Anglia, and this brings me enormous pleasure and more than a little satisfaction. In both cases, time and place took their part. Fate, kismet, karma, destiny, let's say, was at work. No regrets – time and place need to be aligned. But I have never ridden a horse over fences. And I guess I never will. And I regret that. And I guess I always will.

Proverb

A man is not old until his regrets take the place of his dreams.

Abigail Chisman

EDITOR-IN-CHIEF, CONDÉ NAST INTERACTIVE

My parents taught me to try to live without regret, because regret is purely negative and immobilising. The theory I have by heart, but in practice it isn't always quite so easy.

For instance, I find it impossible not to regret hurting other people's feelings. But it's relatively easy to avoid regret over personal failure – not only because I have the unfortunate (though not uncommon) ability to forgive myself faster than I forgive others, but also because it isn't hard to see the benefits of experience: you can only learn from your mistakes if you actually make them. I also believe that, if you can focus on being motivated to change things, disappointment often leads to new opportunities and discoveries.

It's not always possible to see it at the time, however. A helpful trick is to recognise that if you were able to correct past mistakes, you would possibly forfeit present happinesses. For instance, I can't regret the tumultuous saga that my husband and I endured to eventually get to the altar, because a different path might have led to a future that didn't include him and our beautiful daughter, Emerald.

Michael Powell

**CONSULTANT NEUROSURGEON, NATIONAL HOSPITAL
FOR NEUROLOGY AND NEUROSURGERY**

*R*egrets are dangerous things for a surgeon. I hope I always try to do my best, but there is the occasional tricky moment, and even for an experienced surgeon like myself, there are times when things do not go according to plan (let's leave out the details!). So if the surgeon dwells too much on either, 'Could I have taken more of whatever it is out?' or 'Why didn't I leave it be at that?' before something regrettable occurred, then that important surgical optimism gets lost in introspection.

So, no professional regrets! I am happy that I have, in the main, done things that worked and my patients are grateful for my efforts. When things went wrong, being honest and talking about it has allowed me to move on from the less good experiences.

So that leaves regrets outside work. They are a bit trivial as I believe I am lucky in life. Why did I give up playing the classical guitar at university and just before that, why did I not pursue my rock band ambitions after school? Our group could have been contenders! The relaxing distraction of playing music would be wonderful, but in middle age it seems incredibly difficult to relearn and sometimes really frustrating. Distractions in a hard-working life are important, but frustrating distractions I can do without. I have tried classical piano, saxophone, guitar again and even the blues harmonica. Let's face it, I am a wannabe musician with no talent!

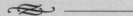

Truman Capote

AUTHOR 1924–1984

My major regret in life is that my childhood was unnecessarily lonely.

Sacha Bonsor

JOURNALIST

I think regret is a fascinating topic, and have been wracking my brains to try and think of something I could say. I think that we probably regret what we don't do, rather that what we do do, and in that respect, due to my relative youth, I suppose I don't yet have many regrets because I still hope I have time to fulfil them! I think a true regret is an irreversible action which, lived again, would be played out differently, and in that sense I find it easier to think in terms of 'mistakes I have made', of which there are plenty.

The one that springs to mind immediately is when I did an interview with a famous author for a newspaper. It was my first big interview, and I was very nervous. She immediately put me at ease, cooked me lunch, and we seemed to be making friends. We chatted about all areas of her life, including her husband's degenerative disease, about which she spoke freely, and which I duly incorporated into the article.

After it was printed, I wrote to her to make sure she liked the piece. She hated it, and both she and her husband were incredibly upset that it had been mentioned. I was mortified, not so much because I had made a mistake, but because if I am being honest, I knew all along that I should not have mentioned it, and did so out of fear and weakness. No good came from it, and if I lived my life again, I would do that differently.

The American philosopher Henry David Thoreau once said, 'To regret deeply is to live afresh.' I suppose, with hindsight, it was an early lesson that integrity should have no sacrifice, and so perhaps in a small sense, good triumphed.

COMEDIAN

On a recent TV programme in which I was marginally involved, a number of celebrities were invited to be interviewed in front of the camera about regrets they had and things they wished they had done differently. Almost without fail, they subtly altered this brief, allowing themselves to lament not their own failures of judgment or courage but instead the short-sightedness and paucity of spirit of those who had thwarted them in their consequently uncompleted endeavours. It rather annoyed me.

It struck me as evasion. Likewise, it would be dishonest to say I 'regret' that my daughter will probably never witness unbleached coral at first hand. It makes me sad, but to 'regret' it is as fraudulent as apologising for slavery or the Peterloo Massacre. It merely diverts attention from my own genuine shortcomings and bad calls. By the end, I almost regretted my involvement in the show. Not quite, though. It took the non-appearance of my travel and accommodation expenses to do that.

It's a tricky business, though, expressing genuine regret. For a start, to acknowledge regret of one's own choices in life would inevitably lead to someone, somewhere, feeling hurt. If I regret not pursuing a certain career, does that mean I would wish unmet the friends I have made along the path I did take? If I regret not kissing a girl I fancied when I was 12, does that show a flaw in the icing of my marriage? (Luckily, there was no girl. You were the first, Kate.)

And regret for a failure to act makes the failure seem final, rather than simply postponed. If I regret not having learned to ski, that means I never shall. It's a resignation. (Although I have never regretted one of those. In fact, I have tendered rather too few.)

Still, there's no getting away from it: irrational and unhelpful though they are, I give regrets plenty of houseroom in thoughts. Regret seems almost the default lens I use for viewing the past – regret or sentimental longing. Pretty unhealthy, no doubt.

Perhaps my overriding regret is my failure to swim more determinedly against the tide. I've always enjoyed acting the rebel, the sceptic, the outsider; in reality I am every bit as in thrall to consumerism, materialism, status symbolism and all the rest of it as anyone else. I regret not having slipped those shackles. I remain convinced that just beneath the wind-buffeted surface of the ocean of modern life there is a deep blue calm I could enjoy – could even coax my family down to join me. We could live like dolphins, slowly shedding our credit facilities, our Boden skin and our obsession with homes-and-property supplements. But I have so far proved incapable of holding my mental breath long enough to resemble any kind of aquatic mammal. If I am ever called a bottlenose, it is for entirely different and less flattering reasons.

Speaking of which, Dean Martin said you're not really drunk if you can lie on the floor without holding on. But of course, if you can lie on the floor without holding on then you are not so much sober as close to enlightenment. If you can pass through an entire day without holding on, I suspect you are probably ready to be rendered blue in allegorical Hindu paintings. I regret not focussing on that goal and instead spending my evenings watching 'reality' TV, which in fact depicts anything but – at least as it would be recognised by anyone who knows what they are talking about.

Then again, I do take comfort from serendipity. A few months ago, I was walking behind a young family in my local park at the perfect distance to be able to spot a teddy being dropped from the pushchair – unnoticed by its owner or her parents – and was able to scoop it up, return it and collect my ransom of smiles and thank yous. Any deviation from my chosen trajectory through life over the previous 42 years and I might not have been there for that moment.

Nevertheless, regrets breed in my head like bacteria in a Petri dish full of juicy agar jelly. Hopefully, some of them will at least provide a compass for the road ahead. I regret at least 90 per cent of the TV I have watched and now watch less than I used to. I regret most of the days I could have spent out walking in the hills but did not – and we are now moving to the country (admittedly with my shoes leaving a cowardly skid mark on the city streets). And I regret, albeit in a pleasant, dull-ache sort of way, every minute that I don't spend picking up my daughter, Matilda, hooking an arm under her genuinely perfect bum and using my free hand to point at squirrels. Especially now that, at only three, she is too big to carry for much more than, say, a mile at a time. Sadly, there are limits to my power to change course. Evasive and dishonest though it may be, I have to say it – I regret that she must grow up.

Dame Kelly Holmes

FORMER MIDDLE-DISTANCE RUNNER AND OLYMPIC MEDAL WINNER

You should never
have regrets, so whatever
you do in life, always give
yourself 100 per cent
chance of succeeding.

John Humphrys

JOURNALIST & BROADCASTER

I wish I'd gone to university. Nobody in my family had gone (in fact, I don't think I knew any students), but I did OK at the eleven-plus and went to a decent grammar school, and I suppose it might have been possible. I was no more stupid than the average child. But my parents didn't have much money (in fact, we were frequently broke) and I suppose I thought I should start earning as quickly as possible. So I left school and joined a local paper when I was 15. I didn't exactly earn a fortune: £1.17s.6d. a week as a trainee reporter. Not that anyone trained me. There was only one other reporter so we did the lot. The expenses were OK: you got your bus fare back, provided you hadn't lost the ticket.

Some say I shouldn't regret not going to university on the basis that I probably wouldn't have done much better if I had. But that's not the point. I've always had a chip on my shoulder about it and I suppose I always will. Maybe that's what makes me such a stroppy sod.

I have a clutch of honorary degrees and have been invited to be a university chancellor, but I turned it down. I'd feel too much of a fraud.

Alexander Graham Bell

INVENTOR OF THE TELEPHONE 1847–1922

When one door closes, another opens;
but we often look so long and so
regretfully upon the closed door that
we do not see the one which has
opened for us.

Georgia Slowe

PLAYS PERDITA HYDE-SINCLAIR IN *EMMERDALE*

*T*o live with regret is a tragedy all of its own. Every day we have to make choices. White or brown bread. A trip to Bognor or Borneo. Each alternative with its own unknown possibilities. We pick out our individual paths through life and then of course we have to live with the consequences, whatever they might be. A bad choice can result in catastrophe, but to then waste precious time and energy on regret is both futile and pointless. It is an emotion with no positive powers; it relentlessly chomps on a painful, unalterable past. Like chewing gum, it gives no nourishment and is ghastly to behold.

We can never be sure how our futures will turn out, or predict the exact way our actions will affect those around us. If you could undo even one small mistake the repercussions might be boundless. Watch *It's a Wonderful Life* and never regret what would have or could have been. Try and find a reason to celebrate the wonders in your life and leave the regrets with the mistakes, far behind you.

Alastair Campbell

**FORMER DIRECTOR OF COMMUNICATIONS AND STRATEGY
FOR THE LABOUR PARTY**

I wish I had read more books when I had the time, namely at university. Barely a day goes by when I don't see a book and say to myself, 'I wish I had read that.' It then goes on my list of books to read, but so many new books come on the market which I also feel I should read, and the list of the unread gets longer and longer.

I spent a lot of time socialising and generally messing about at university. The time I devoted to books and study went purely on my subject, modern languages, and within that, virtually exclusively on the books we really had to study. So I feel I had a fantastic opportunity to broaden my horizons through literature, didn't really take it, and have never caught up.

Once you get into the world of work, and then raising a family, there never seems to be enough time, though I now spend time once given over to reading newspapers on reading books, and if I ever retire, I intend to have a structured reading programme, starting with every book ever written by Balzac and Flaubert, and the auto-biographies of every British prime minister and US president.

Peter Bowles

ACTOR

I was sitting rather exhausted and drained in a pub after two performances of *Present Laughter*. A waiter came over and asked if he could get me something – I asked him to please bring me a ham sandwich and a pint of beer. The beer arrived with the message that the sandwich would soon follow. A man suddenly appeared before me in a torn T-shirt and jeans and said, 'Please forgive the interruption but I am a huge fan of yours and would love it if you could join me and my girl for supper – we are just across the road and saw you come in here. Oh, forgive me, my name is Quentin Tarantino.'

In true English style I said, 'That's so kind of you [fearing I was going to upset the waiter or something!] but I have just ordered a sandwich.'

'OK! Rain check – love your work!' said Mr Tarantino and left.

I munched my sandwich thinking I must be mad apart from being perhaps a little standoffish to an American visitor, and I had the film rights and the script of *Gangster No. 1* (for which I was executive producer) sitting in my briefcase.

Well, I did get the film made eventually – but who knows how things would have turned out if I'd had supper with Mr Tarantino, who at that time had just made his first film, *Reservoir Dogs*.

Frederick Forsyth
AUTHOR

*E*ven after 68 years' pootling round this planet, one of my regrets occurred only about a year ago.

The lovely Gloria Hunniford had been asked to take part in *Who Wants to Be a Millionaire?* and she had asked me to partner her. She was competing for her own cancer charity and I had chosen a small group who raise money for children with cerebral palsy.

At first things went like a dream. Question after question just happened to be something that jogged a chord of memory. At £32,000 we hit a stinker, a sporting question. The audience response was equivocal, though we had hoped for a huge percentage with the right answer. Our 'phone a friend' had not a clue either. We used the last lifeline, 50/50, and got it right – but all safety nets were gone.

Then the brilliant luck returned and we shot to £250,000. The half-million pound question was: what is the shortest book in the Old Testament? Ruth, Amos, Micah or Obadiah? I was pretty damn sure it was Obadiah... say, 80 per cent. Gloria pointed out we would lose £218,000 if we were wrong and that the money now really belonged to cancer victims and children in wheelchairs. Not ours to gamble.

So we quit. It *was* Obadiah. I will as long as I live regret that I did not put my money where my big mouth was and insist on Obadiah, and be prepared to cough up if I were wrong. But I bottled out.

I still lie awake trying to relive it all but taking that question and getting it right. And wondering what the million-pound question would have been. And if we could have won half a million each for our charities instead of £125,000.

And if it had been Micah (my second choice) after all? I would have lost £218,000, but I would prefer that to the bruises I collect from kicking myself for losing my nerve.

Roddy Llewellyn

HORTICULTURIST, JOURNALIST AND AUTHOR

*T*wo small changes to one word of Frank Sinatra's song portray my regret for not having enough tucked away for my dotage:

'Regrets, I've had a few. But then again, too few to pension.'

Alan Whicker

BROADCASTER AND AUTHOR

I have always wished that I had taken the

time to become a song-and-dance man – in

the Fred Astaire mould, you understand.

Being slightly tone deaf could surely be

overcome with the right backing, and those

enormous swooping flights of white stairs

could then be taken on the hoof, in my

Whicker's World stride.

Anna Massey
ACTRESS

I have regretted many things that I have done in my life, but they seem to me to have been on the whole trivial and unimportant compared with the things I have not done. Alas, this list is long and makes me realise how timid and unintrepid I have been. I have travelled very little in my later years. I have never climbed mountains, or sailed the seven seas. But what I regret most of all is that I never learnt another language, so that I could speak it as fluently as my own.

I learnt French at school, and for a year I lived with a family in Paris. This enabled me to acquire quite a passable accent, and to converse on a very superficial level. But I would love to have acquired a large vocabulary, one that would have allowed me to read the great French authors in their original texts, and not to have to rely on good translators. So much is lost in translation. While watching French films I am forced to read the subtitles, and thereby lose so many subtleties. You cannot immerse yourself in another country's culture without a profound knowledge of their language. Therefore I know that I have missed many treats and pleasures, which with more effort and perspicacity when young would have enriched my life in many ways. This is one of my chief regrets.

Ernest Hemingway

AUTHOR 1899–1961

Only one marriage I regret. I
remember after I got that
marriage licence I went across
from the licence bureau to a bar
for a drink. The bartender said,
'What will you have, sir?' And
I said, 'A glass of hemlock.'

John Hardy

PROFESSOR OF NEUROSCIENCE, INSTITUTE OF NEUROLOGY

Of course, I am sure everybody looks back and thinks about how things might have turned out, if they had made other decisions. They consider their alternative lives, and I am no different from others in that regard. I don't know if those really count as regrets: certainly, I am a happy person, and seeing my kids thrive in their own lives is as much as anyone could ask.

There are some things I wish I had done, though: I wish I had had the courage to take a year off, either before I went to university or, probably better, between doing my degree and starting my PhD. I did consider taking a year out and doing something different: going to Africa or to Southeast Asia and doing something useful, but I didn't quite have the courage, and after that, after I had started my PhD., I was really on the treadmill. Since then, I feel never really to have had the opportunity to take time away.

My other regret is similar: I love street food, the local snacks sold by the side of the road, out of shopfronts or off carts, cheap. Everywhere has their own: hot dogs in New York, fish and chips in England, kebabs in Turkey, but far more varied and exotic in Southeast Asia. I always wanted to take a year off and write a book about this snack food: going from place to place, taking a picture of the vendor and the shopfront or food cart, and writing a few words about the vendor, with a recipe and picture of the food. It is sadly too late, as type II diabetes means such a year would probably kill me, so I write this in the hope that someone else will also think this is a good idea and have fun with it instead.

Taiwan is the best place I have been for street food, but I have been told Vietnam and Thailand are better. What a treat to find out…

Eric Sykes

ACTOR AND AUTHOR

I have had several regrets in my life, several things which I did not do, and the biggest regret I have now is that I can't remember any of them.

Lord Owen

FORMER LEADER OF THE SDP

I am often asked 'Do I regret giving up medicine?' In truth, I never really gave up medicine. I fought the constituency of Torrington, North Devon, in 1964 but it only involved going there one weekend a month and the only question was whether I could save my deposit. In 1966 I stood for the city in which I was born, Plymouth. It was a marginal seat but I never really believed I could win it. Even a week before polling day I was surprised when an MP travelling with the then prime minister, Harold Wilson, said, 'See you in Westminster.' Sensing my surprise he added, 'You had better get used to it. You will be an MP in a week's time!'

I always put down winning to my father's patients voting for me out of respect for him, since part of his GP practice lay in the constituency. I returned to my laboratory in the Medical Unit of St Thomas's Hospital having taken three weeks' unpaid leave to fight the Election. I was working with Dr David Marsden using the tremor of the fingers to investigate the effects of adrenergic beta-blocker drugs. David went on to become a distinguished Professor of Neurology at the National Hospital. I simply crossed over Westminster Bridge, continuing to work in the Medical Unit every morning and sometimes not going over to the House of Commons until the late afternoon. I was still ambivalent about what was my prime activity – medicine or politics.

Then suddenly in 1968 the decision was taken out of my hands. Harold Wilson invited me into his Government as Under-Secretary of State for the Royal Navy. When the Election was called in 1970, fearing defeat I began to look in the *BMJ* (*British*

Medical Journal) for posts in neuropsychiatry and I was particularly keen to go to the Maudsley. Against all the odds, with neighbouring Labour MPs losing their seats in Exeter and Falmouth, I managed to hold on to mine. Immediately after the Election I was asked to become part-time chairman of an American company, Decision Technology, one of whose clients was Hoffman Le Roche. This started a relationship with the pharmaceutical industry which I maintained when I became Minister of Health in 1974 and was the sponsoring minister for the industry. For two and a half years it was the best job I ever held.

In the 1979 General Election, having been Foreign Secretary for two and a half years, I contemplated defeat and once again turned to the *BMJ*. But this time I began to doubt that I could really return to medicine. Holding my seat meant I was pitched into the fight to save the Labour Party from committing itself to unilateral nuclear disarmament and withdrawal from the European Community without even a referendum. We lost that battle and I helped found the SDP. Only in the 1980s did I cease to call myself a medical practitioner when filling in details of my occupation. I became involved in medicine again in 1996, as a director of an American pharmaceutical company, Abbott Laboratories, and continue to serve on the Board.

I think, therefore, I can fairly claim that I have never entirely left medicine. But there has never been a period in my life longer than a month when some article, some event or some chance conversation has brought back a feeling of regret that I was no longer practising medicine.

Sir Michael Holroyd

AUTHOR AND BIOGRAPHER

I was in the middle of writing a really difficult sentence when a national newspaper rang me out of the blue and asked whether I would agree to be flown the next day to the United States to cover the heavyweight boxing championship of the world. Having made sure that this was not a practical joke, I prepared to give them a resounding yes – and heard myself quietly say no.

What could have been my reason? Was it that difficult sentence or simply a failure of nerve? A couple of days later I watched the match on television and saw two bulky lads dancing round each other, pawing and cuddling – even lying down once or twice. It was a poignant scene and I could have made much of it. And it might have changed my career – I might even have had a pension by now (forty years of pension would be most useful now). As it was, I merely went back to wrestle with that difficult sentence, full of regret.

Oscar Wilde

PLAYWRIGHT, NOVELIST AND POET 1854–1900

Most people die of a sort of creeping common sense, and discover when it is too late that the only things one never regrets are one's mistakes.

Quentin Letts

JOURNALIST

*U*p goes the wail in the middle of the night and there's a sort of game of chicken in the marital bed. We know we're both awake but who is going to get up to settle the baby? Ugh, how old I feel, knackered like an ancient dobbin. Finally: 'I'll go.' Knee joints creak as I swing them over the side of the bed. Then – aiee! – I step on a sharp nugget of Lego in the corridor and – thud! – hit my head on one of the beams and – twanggg! – catch my finger in the clasp of the cot. It's like a bleeding Inspector Clouseau film, and 'bleeding' is the word.

What do I regret? Not getting married 10 years earlier and having our adored children when we were still in our twenties. Instead, like many of our generation, we left it until our mid-thirties, by which time the crows' feet were starting to nest and the energy levels were dregs swilling round the bottom of the tea cup.

Parenthood is a youngsters' game. Just thinking about that woman of 60 who gave birth the other day makes me yawn with tiredness on her behalf.

Waiter! Another glass of your finest Sanatogen, at the double.

AUTHOR

For half a century and more I have regretted that instead of embarking on a comfortable writing career of non-fiction, wanly tinged with the imaginative, I did not go the whole hog from the start, shack up in a loft somewhere and live a bold, indigent life writing novels. They might have been flops, and I probably would not have enjoyed that penniless attic, but at least I would have tried!

Sir Matthew Pinsent

FORMER ROWER & OLYMPIC MEDAL WINNER

The only regret I have, and it's not a big one in the scheme of things, is not pursuing a musical instrument. My parents put me through a few piano lessons and were devastated when I decided for purely lazy reasons that I shouldn't continue it. I wasn't any good and showed no promise of being anything other than average, but a little bit of me always wants to sit down at a piano and be able to play something apart from 'Chopsticks'!

Grayson Perry

TURNER PRIZE-WINNING ARTIST

---

*R*egret is not something that I don't feel very often; as an artist my motto is 'creativity is mistakes'.

My most common regret comes to mind when I stare into the mirror as I am about to put on my make-up. I think about how thin and smooth I was when I was young, how thick my long blond hair was, and how I never made the most of my youthful good looks. I skulked about in drab dresses trying to blend in, when what I needed was to sashay and strut and flirt. If I put my hair in a ponytail then, it was as thick as my wrist; now it is more of a pencil.

I didn't have the confidence to dress up then as I do today, now I am wrinkled and sagging and losing my hair. When I was 20 I made a lovely girl but I was too frightened to enjoy it properly. I wish at 46 I could talk to my 20-year-old self and tell him what I have learnt too late. If I am happy and confident being a man swanning about in a dress, then pretty well everyone around me will feel the same. Nervousness is contagious. I would tell myself 'you look lovely' and 'if they laugh, laugh with them'. I wish I had put on a sexy, short red dress and high heels and strolled through the centre of town drawing all kinds of stares.

Richard Wilson

ACTOR

Some days I regret not going to university and some days I am glad I didn't, but the one thing I do regret is that I didn't nourish my brain more when I was younger – that I didn't read more, that I didn't seek more, that I didn't make more use of this extraordinary instrument.

On the other hand, I try not to have too many regrets as it's a counterproductive, idle activity.

Lord Steel

FORMER LEADER OF THE LIBERAL PARTY

In 1952, five days before she became Queen, Princess Elizabeth and the Duke of Edinburgh visited the new St Andrew's Church of Scotland, Nairobi, for which my father as its Minister had been responsible. As a 13-year-old boy I had a ringside seat by the table outside the door where they were to sign the visitors' book. I took pictures of them with my Box Brownie camera. Afterwards I nicked the blotting paper they had used, which when held up to a mirror clearly showed the two signatures: 'Elizabeth' and 'Philip'.

I took it to show off at school and swapped it for two white mice, which I named Elizabeth and Philip and who later turned into 60 white mice, but I lost the precious piece of paper bearing our future Queen's signature.

Simon Williams

ACTOR

I have done things I ought not to have done and I have left undone things I ought to have done. They are almost too numerous, but hey, I'm 60 and it's the decade of regret.

Mostly I regret taking life at such a rush. Why did I always want to be a grown-up when, from where I sit now, it looks as though childhood is a place to tarry in for as long as possible? Always I've eschewed the idea of 'sleeping on things' – I've always made impulsive decisions, rash ones.

Why do I never read the instruction manual before plugging in a new appliance? Why do I so often leap in feet first without weighing up the pros and cons? Why do I/did I sometimes not listen carefully enough? Especially to my parents and grandparents and now to my children and grandchildren.

Why have I not taken to heart those lovely simple lines of W.H. Davies? 'What is this life if, full of care, we have no time to stand and stare?'

Arthur Miller

PLAYWRIGHT 1915–2005

Maybe all
one can
do is hope
to end
up with
the
right
regrets.

Wendy Craig

ACTRESS

I don't belong to the 'no regrets' brigade. There are indeed things I regret, and I'm afraid I'm becoming too long in the tooth to redeem many of them. However, there is one regret I am determined to address. I wish I had continued learning French when I left school. One feels so left out of things when invited to an exciting dinner party with guests from the Continent, or at some grand cosmopolitan event where I'm longing to take part in a stimulating conversation but instead am left desperately concentrating, yet embarrassingly speechless.

Then there is so much wonderful French literature to be read, and films and plays to watch without the need for subtitles. Wouldn't it be splendid, when in France, to be able to speak to people in restaurants and shops without being received with supercilious Gallic shrugs?

Well, help is now at hand in the form of teaching CDs, two of which arrived free in a daily newspaper. Now all I need is some precious free time to recommence my studies, then *voilà*! Another regret dispensed with – together with computer literacy, learning to play the piano, reading *War and Peace*, and so on… well, no, I'll deal with those later.

Anna Raeburn

JOURNALIST AND BROADCASTER

---

*T*o regret is to open the door to misgiving. I prefer to think first rather than to regret afterwards. And most of the things I regret are beyond my power to influence.

I regret I wasn't born rich; I spend money to better effect than most of the people I know. I regret I didn't earlier embrace my mother's excellent advice: 'Just be yourself'. I am sorry I wasn't born a better person, brighter, taller, slimmer, green-eyed and with a waist. But at least I no longer dress that person.

I wish I were kinder but I don't regret not being. Jenny Tonge deeply impressed me when she responded at a public meeting, 'I am sorry if I displeased you but not sorry I said what I meant.' I regret the people I have hurt or disappointed. I regret I can't go back again and explain what I was trying to achieve.

I regret the way the consumer society has caused such destruction in every way, and the unholy development of David Shepherd's idea of a two nation society – the haves and the have-nots and the chasm of broken glass between them. I also regret the BBC *Nine O'Clock News* being moved. I regret change even as I acknowledge its inevitability.

But I don't regret very much. And I regret that I don't regret very much. Because I'd like to have a great secret regret that I could offer this book – and then it might cause a furore, the exploitation of which would focus attention on an important cause. But no. I have tried to live life as it comes.

Stuart Hall

PROFESSOR OF CULTURAL THEORY AND SOCIOLOGY

Ever since I was diagnosed with end-term renal failure in 1982, I have been in the care of, and now in weekly treatment by, the NHS. I am enormously grateful for all it has done for me, especially the care and attention of those who labour in its wards; though contact with it, as is the case with all such enormous bureaucracies, can be irritating and deeply frustrating. Of course, a complex system like this needs huge public investment (though not at the cost of allowing private interests to cherry-pick and hollow it out from the inside); it needs to be managed well (though not at the expense of clinical judgements); it needs public health priorities to meet (though not at the behest of an ever-expanded target culture), and there are a thousand daily choices to make between competing goods which have to be balanced one against another. However, I never turn up for my regular dialysis sessions – with their typical cross-section of patients drawn from the multicultural London of which we used to be proud but which is now progressively falling into disrepute – without thinking of the great idea that has informed it from the beginning, and thanking my lucky stars for its existence, despite all its many failings. Without the enormous advances in medical treatment now available to everyone through the NHS, I would not have survived. And without the NHS I could never have afforded it.

Especially, it makes me reflect on how against the odds and exceptional the very conception of the NHS is. 'Free at the point of delivery', and as a right, in this entrepreneurial age, is the critical dimension that touches the lives and relieves the anxiety and the suffering of everyone. But more significant is its underlying philosophy. The very idea of de-coupling the primordial link between health care and personal wealth, which drove the NHS at its founding – that 'to each according to their needs' should become the governing principle of a public institution – stops us in our tracks.

Richard Titmuss once argued that the logic which appropriately guides the NHS is not that of 'the market' but of the 'gift' relationship, whose model is the unselfish practice of blood donorship. This is like throwing one's bread upon the water without knowing exactly if or when we will personally benefit from it; not because we want to ensure that enough is available for *us* when we need it, but because, in a larger sense, we are all connected with, dependent on and responsible for one another, in that wider but unpopular sense which we can only call *social*. This idea is so bold, so *radical* in the proper sense of the word, and above all so out of sync with the very grain and ethos of public thinking today, that its survival in institutional form is, to be honest, astonishing.

The survival of the idea of the de-commodification of health – which is what it is – in an era when everything has to become a commodity, in a market, in order to acquire 'value', is itself quite unpredictable. The idea of an 'economy of needs' whose product is not distributed according to individual capacity to buy it, is now so old-fashioned a conception, so contrary to the 'logic' that has become singularly dominant as we 'modernise' ourselves from an 'old fashioned' welfare state into the new market state, that it would be literally *unthinkable* today if it did not already exist. Imagine the scorn with which such a notion would be greeted: by the political forces now all gathered in the middle ground of politics, disputing like angels on the head of a pin; by the economists of the Treasury or the CBI, who are driven by the singular goal of economic efficiency; by the sceptical tribe of *The Times* or the *Today* programme, to whom the logic of privatisation has become so ubiquitous, so taken for granted, that no serious question can be framed, no debate predicated, no interview conducted or news story designed on the basis of any other proposition; by the corporate rich, increasingly enfranchised within the state, whose birth-right it is to buy themselves out of anything that is so common as to be public – available to everybody. 'There is no such thing as society; there is only the individual and his family.' This is the governing principle and watchword of the modern age.

So that when, at a point of serious, sudden or unexpected illness, as was the case recently with our beloved daughter, one comes across a hospital of the highest excellence, like the National Hospital for Neurology and Neurosurgery – where the quality of care and the atmosphere of personal attention are quite extraordinary even for the NHS, where the most advanced medical technology is available in the genuine context of care and concern, and there is a supportive system that is flexible enough to be adapted to individual need – it puts one in mind of the ancient concept of the hospital: a hospitable place of care for the ill as an obligation and duty in its own right. Here staff put their extraordinary expertise at the service of the patient and their families, to comfort their fears and anxieties, and to speak honestly and directly to them, without false hope or patronage. This cannot help but make one think that the 'trace' of another life, a different way of thinking and behaving, another conception of society, is not yet quite extinct: indeed, in such places, is still quite miraculously alive. How deeply I regret that this is rarely the case.

A List of Contributors

Esther Rantzen 145

Claire Rayner 138

Corin Redgrave 46

Ian Rickson 46

Angela Rippon 8

Lord Rix 77

Jon Ronson 37

Royal Marines Commando 103

Oliver Sacks 19

Sir Jimmy Savile 4

Prunella Scales 5

Hannah Shields 62

Peter Shilton 55

Simon Shorvon 114

Jeffrey Siegel 100

Alan Sillitoe 18

Georgia Slowe 160

Tim Smit 76

Gareth Southgate 69

Lord Steel 179

Lord Stevens 126

Lord Stevenson 42

Nobby Stiles 35

Una Stubbs 32

Meera Syal 129

Eric Sykes 169

Ray Tallis 128

Lord Tebbit 54

Emma Tennant 99

Kate Thornton 136

Alan Titchmarsh 129

Lynne Truss 130

Sir Mark Tully 121

Terry Waite 22

Matthew Walker 55

Pete Waterman 96

Arabella Weir 113

Sir Arnold Wesker 88

Alan Whicker 165

Ann Widdecombe 95

Rowan Williams 5

Simon Williams 180

Richard Wilson 178

Antony Worrall Thompson 35

Benjamin Zephaniah 29